Getting Out

Getting Out

A Restorative Approach to Prison Ministry

MICHAEL B. BOWE

RESOURCE *Publications* • Eugene, Oregon

GETTING OUT
A Restorative Approach to Prison Ministry

Copyright © 2020 Michael B. Bowe. All rights reserved. Except for brief
quotations in critical publications or reviews, no part of this book may
be reproduced in any manner without prior written permission from the
publisher. Write: Permissions, Wipf and Stock Publishers, 199 W. 8th Ave.,
Suite 3, Eugene, OR 97401.

Resource Publications
An Imprint of Wipf and Stock Publishers
199 W. 8th Ave., Suite 3
Eugene, OR 97401

www.wipfandstock.com

PAPERBACK ISBN: 978-1-7252-6626-1
HARDCOVER ISBN: 978-1-7252-6627-8
EBOOK ISBN: 978-1-7252-6628-5

Manufactured in the U.S.A.   MAY 21, 2020

To my family

Contents

CHAPTER 1

Overview

INTRODUCTION TO THE PROBLEM AND PURPOSE OF THIS MINISTRY PROJECT

I NEVER IMAGINED THAT I would be involved with prison ministry. Moreover, I would never have thought my overall ministry would go in the direction it went. Unfortunately, I created issues and barriers that have limited but shaped my ministry. In 2010, I plead guilty to my first felony. I subsequently lost my job and had trouble finding new work. I still had all the expenses of before, but now I was a convicted felon. Therefore, I reoffended again and again. Finally, I ended up in prison. My failure was a result of poor planning and not relying on family help available. I felt I had no choice. Yet, that was not the case. While there are problems in the social system, I came to recognize that my crimes were against myself and the system. When released, I recognized I did not want to return to prison. However, I ran into more trouble finding work than ever before. I recognized that I was certainly not alone and these problems and many others need to be considered within ministry.

My initial personal experience with prison ministry, while I was in prison, was enlightening. But not enlightening the way the prison ministry probably had hoped. I found the programs that were offered to inmates to be limited and solely focused on salvation or conversion. Many people would parole out or end their sentence and would face all the problems I encountered and more. Many people did not have the resources I had available. Furthermore, I recognized many inmates were not prepared to reenter society. Unfortunately, many of the people who exit prison reoffend and will reenter. This is not the life God intended for anyone. What exists as prison ministry today has to go further. It has to better equip people to address the social system to which the person will be returning. I hope to contribute to that effort. I wanted to create an approach to ministry that will foster a balance between individual responsibility with regard to sin, crime, and wrong doing, along with addressing the social responsibilities necessary to restore the persons incarcerated as a productive member of society.

CONTEXT

Something needs to be done to address some of the problems people face when transitioning out of incarceration. This book proposes a restorative prison ministry that engages an expanded approach that will draw upon the social gospel, restorative justice, and a communal contextual model of pastoral care, primarily utilizing concepts in Bowen Family Systems Theory in order to more effectively address offender reentry into society. In developing this approach, I will criticize the traditional model of prison ministry that focuses on the individualistic gospel that favors retributive justice and relies upon an individualistic model of clinical pastoral care. I wish to answer the question: Is recidivism the result of a "failure of nerve"[1] in high anxiety or high pressure situations and would a communal contextual pastoral care approach focusing on restorative justice and the social gospel lower the recidivism rate?

1. Friedman, *Failure of Nerve.*

UNDERSTANDING THE PROBLEM

How can prison ministries better equip someone leaving prison to face the challenges those newly released face? This book focuses on the Alabama department of corrections (ADOC) and persons in Alabama. There are a lot of problems within the ADOC. People are being released back into society unprepared for the challenges they will face. Unfortunately, prison ministries are not helping people convicted of crimes beyond individual pastoral care and salvation. Regrettably, there is not a recidivism statistic specifically for those involved in prison ministry programs. Instead, the only information available is the ADOC's reported overall recidivism rate of 31.5%[2] This writing will address the ADOC's problems with overcrowding, recidivism, and the failure of individual pastoral care within prison ministry for people transitioning out of prison.

OVERCROWDED

Prisons in Alabama are overpopulated. The ADOC is overwhelmed with the number of incarcerated persons. In their 2017 annual report, the ADOC reported a population of 27,803 inmates, 21,213 are in an actual prison. The remaining are either in a contract bed in another facility, serving time in another state, or involved in a supervised release program.[3] These statistics does not include people on probation, or in county or city jails awaiting their day in court. National trends seem worse. "As of 2011, more than 7.3 million adults in the United States are under some form of supervision by state, local, or federal criminal justice systems, including probation, jail, prison, and parole."[4] The data is quite clear, the criminal justice system has a far reach both nationally as well as statewide.

2. There will be further discussion concerning redivisim and the ADOC's reported rate on pages 4–6.

3. ADOC. "Annual Report Fiscal Year 2017.

4. Levad, "I was in prison and you visited me' *Journal Of The Society Of Christian Ethics*, 93–112.

Traditional prison ministry is overwhelmed by the sheer number of people incarcerated within the ADOC. While traditional prison ministry makes an effort to build relationships with each individual, it is incredibly difficult. Therefore, the various traditional prison ministries take an easier approach that focuses solely on the incarcerated individual's salvation. Traditional prison ministries usually come to the prison and leads various worship services that focus on a broad look at sin, and how God can save prisoners from their wretched lives. This approach cheapens grace because it focuses on obvious issues and offers a simple solution that doesn't promise much change.

RECIDIVISM

This is an alternative approach to prison ministry that may help with recidivism. Recidivism happens when people released from prison do not have adequate resources available to function in society. So they relapse into previous dysfunctional or destructive behavior and return to prison. Alabama is recognizing their current correctional system is broken. Their facilities are outdated and in ill repair, and overcrowded. These problems are well known. In a news report, the ADOC commissioner, Jeff Dunn stated, "Alabama's prison facilities are not conducive to educational and treatment programs needed to prepare inmates for their eventual release from prison. He said 95 percent of prisoners will return to their communities."[5] In that same story, as he was petitioning for better facilities, he mentioned that the department is unequipped to provide the care inmates need to transition out.[6] In their annual report, ADOC reveal 14,200 people were released from the ADOC. However, this number includes escapes and death.[7] Unfortunately, no matter how fast the criminal justice system grows, it does not seem to be effective in reducing crime or producing

5. Cason, Alabama will build 3 prisons for men, 2019, February 12.
6. Cason, Alabama will build 3 prisons for men, 2019, February 12.
7. ADOC, "Annual Report Fiscal Year 2017."

offenders capable and able to re-enter society as productive members. Alabama reports a 31.5% recidivism rate.[8] The recidivism statistic does not take into consideration people on probation that reoffend. Moreover, it does not consider people with lesser misdemeanor charges that reoffend. It only considers people entered into the ADOC that within 3 years of release either on parole, alternative sentencing, or end of sentence, and reoffend.

What causes recidivism? Why is the statistic so high? Reentry is difficult. Byran Stevenson, founder of Equal Justice Initiative, indicates one problem, "My state of Alabama, like a number of states, actually permanently disenfranchises you if you have a criminal conviction."[9] The system not only disenfranchise people, it finds a way to keep people indebted to the system and trapped in it. There are a number of problems in the justice system that help people become repeat offenders. These problems create a number of challenges for the transitioning prisoner.

First, this newly freed individual must find a place to live. This can be quite difficult without considerable savings, or family support. Work Release is hardly a relief in Alabama. The ADOC requires 40% of income earned be paid to the department. Then restitution and child support is withheld, often leaving inmates with nothing. However, if the family is not available or unwilling to help, there are some limited means with halfway houses and homeless shelters.

There are also challenges finding suitable work. First, the educational irregularities of the majority of inmates is a major problem in gaining employment. "The ADOC reports a 5th grade average education for male and female inmates within the system."[10] Second, many places will have closed doors and will not want to take the risks involved in hiring someone with a criminal record, including people with certain skills and education. These job related struggles create financial difficulties. There are jobs

---

8. ADOC, "Annual Report Fiscal Year 2017.".

9. Stevenson, Transcript of "We need to talk about an injustice".

10. ADOC, "Annual Report Fiscal Year 2017".

available, but the opportunities are certainly limited by these factors. These difficulties shape and create issues with recidivism.

FAILURE OF INDIVIDUAL PASTORAL CARE

Traditional prison ministry in Alabama has not offered much to help address the concerns of transition and recidivism. In most cases, these ministries involve going into a prison system and building a relationship with a group of inmates in order to share the gospel during a chapel service. This individual salvation focused prison ministry comes in many forms and these relationships are built by various means. Unfortunately, the relationships built during prison ministry visits often become short term relationships. "Mainstream people who are generally morally correct are often afraid of people who habitually break the law and the established moral rules."[11] Inside the prison, everything is controlled. However, once someone leaves prison, people disengage. It is not intentional, but there is a disconnect once a person leaves prison. These ministries are often limited to someone's confinement. The unfortunate end result of this limited scope of ministry can bring a negative reaction to God, church, and ministry.

Most traditional prison ministries are very limited in their focus. This focus is solely on individual conversion, such as "accepting Jesus as Savior." There are a limited number that will offer some of the state sanctioned programming in order to be recognized by the courts. However, in each of these programs and ministries, there are some common elements: individual treatment, retributive justice, and a lack of account for the social system.

DEFINING THE PROBLEM

The ADOC and traditional prison ministry in Alabama have something in common. They both work on a very limited focus. Traditional prison ministry in Alabama remains focused on the

11. Ekblad, *Reading the Bible with the Damned*, xv.

individual, his or her crime, and his or her individual salvation. These traditional prison ministries follow a system of retributive justice, like the ADOC.[12] A person who commits a crime must be punished. However, the problem is far more complex. Therefore, this text focuses on analyzing both individual pastoral care and retributive justice and their limitations for persons transitioning out of prison before offering the alternative of a systems approach grounded in the social gospel and restorative justice.

ANALYSIS OF INDIVIDUAL PASTORAL CARE

Historically, pastoral care has primarily followed a clinical model. Nancy Ramsey describes a historical model of pastoral care stating, "The clinical pastoral perspective . . . is more clinically focused on relationally conceived selves in the immediacy of their lived experience with their social context often in the background."[13] This type of pastoral care has dominated much of prison ministry. It is focused primarily on the individual inmate and his or her crime. The care provider may meet with the family but it is to provide support, care, and possible additional insight to the inmate considered as a problem. This meeting with the family is sometimes called family counseling. However, the lynchpin is the "problemed person." "Family members are seen in order to help them cope with a problem in another family member."[14] Individual pastoral care attempts to treat a crisis. It makes the gospel prescriptive and ineffective by cheapening grace, and remaining individually focused on the inmate's wrongdoing.

This limited scope of pastoral care trims the gospel to an individualized focus which fits all too well with a mainstream society that consistently rejects people who have been convicted of crimes. Bob Ekblad, a minister who reflects a more social gospel sums up the result of this individual method of ministry, "Many people

12. See Appendix: "Current State of Alabama Prison Ministries" for more information about difficulties with ADOC and traditional prison ministry.

13. Ramsay, *Pastoral care and counseling,* 9.

14. Friedman, *Generation to generation,* 22–23.

lose hope in God or have given up even discussing together their disappointments. Jesus, God and the church may as well be dead to them."[15] The salvation that was offered as a great deliverance in prison is found wanting. Individual salvation does not mean much when rent is due. Individual salvation does not help someone find reasonable paying work. Individual salvation does not solve family dysfunction. Unfortunately, individual salvation is all prison ministries offer to address people transitioning out of prison. Notsurprisingly, it has not been much help reducing recidivism.

Alabama utilizes other programs besides prison ministry to treat recidivism. However, each program is focused on the individual and his or her failure. These programs include, drug treatment programs, mental health care, trade training, and a variety of social classes. However, these programs are understaffed and are very limited in resources. Jonathan Simon writes about civil cases against other prisons in *Mass Incarceration on Trial*, where these prisons had to face reforms based on the limited resources. Alabama will likely fall in a similar category with deteriorating facilities, limited resources, and understaffing.

Alabama does utilize outside prison resources for people transitioning back into society. The parole board, in conjunction with ADOC, utilizes several programs for people transitioning out of prison. These programs are: Daily Report Centers (in certain counties), Certain Enforcement Supervision, Moral Reconation Therapy (MRT), Cognitive Behavior Interventions for Substance abuse, LIFE Tech, and L.I.F.E institute.[16] While people meet in group settings, these approaches follow individual therapy and neglect the full social system and how it shapes people. Moreover, these approaches offer general or canned resources intended to cause an individual to rethink his or her choices.

15. Ekblad, *Reading the Bible with the Damned*, 1.

16. Alabama Board of Pardons and Paroles, "Annual Report Fiscal Year 2018".

ANALYSIS OF RETRIBUTIVE JUSTICE

The problems with overcrowding, recidivism, and individualistic prison ministry are all connected with an approach to criminal justice that reflects a retributive approach. The entire justice system in Alabama and most other states is based upon retributive justice. Retributive justice focuses on punishment for the individual. Kathrine Getek Soltis explains, "In the traditional justice paradigm of retribution, the primary concern is to determine what the offender deserves, thereby focusing on guilt with an orientation toward the past."[17] Retributive justice systems do not consider the complexity of the person who committed the crime. Recognizing the complexity of the person does not diminish the wrong, or neglect punishment. However, it takes into consideration all the factors at play in a person's involvement with criminal activity.

For example, crime may be driven by economic climates. When the economy is down, and wages are kept low, crime goes up. E. Britt Patterson, assistant professor of criminology and criminal justice at Florida State University, did a study on crime and poverty. "The findings indicate that absolute poverty is more strongly associated with neighborhood crime rates."[18] It feeds into the age old ethical dilemma: would you steal a loaf of bread to feed your family? However, economic conditions are not the only crime initiator. There are also mental defects that are hardly accounted for in the criminal justice system. Instead, there is a farce medical test, often asking competency questions, to determine understanding between right and wrong. Mental health is a new science and psychotropic medications are always evolving. Yet, the criminal justice system does not take these advancements into consideration within its own system. Additionally, crime is sometimes motivated by family dysfunction. A family is filled with complex, dynamic relationships that shape each of us. However, these family

17. Getek,"Mass incarceration and theological images of justice" *Journal of the Society of Christian Ethics,* 113–130.

18. Patterson,"Poverty, Income Inequality, And Community Crime Rates." *Criminology,* 755–776.

influences can be both positive and negative. The criminal justice system neglects these and other facets. Instead, it remains steadfast in its form of punishment of the individual convicted of wrongdoing. Yet, the retributive justice system is continuing to prove itself ineffective.

Retributive justice is often viewed as the biblical model for justice. C.S. Lewis is noted for his essay on the subject entitled, "The Humanitarian Theory of Punishment."[19] In this essay, Lewis argues that the punishment is what restores the human. "Lewis' great fear is that, if the medical model (the criminal is sick) replaces the guilt model (the criminal deserves punishment), then all kinds of tyranny may follow."[20] Unfortunately, the person who has committed a crime, may be sick. Additionally, Lewis ignores that there may be other social factors involved in the offender's life. Retributive justice does not consider these specific factors because it focuses on the individual and the wrongdoing. It only considers the crime, the victim, and attempts to enact a just punishment. Thus it contributes to recidivism by focusing on guilt and punishment rather than restoration. It also contributes to an individualistic prison ministry by focusing on the criminal act in isolation from the total life of the offender and his or her relation to a community

Retributive justice systems claims to deter crime. If the punishment is harsh enough, people will not want to commit the crime. "In retributive justice, a fit and measured response of good or evil is distributed among human beings in accordance with what their own actions deserve—good for good and evil for evil."[21] Alabama's justice system employs this approach. Alabama seeks to punish an offender for his or her actions in such a way so that the person offending does not want to do it again, and anyone else does not want to suffer the same fate. Notwithstanding, crimes are

19. Cole, "Justice: retributive or reformatitive?" *The Reformed Theological Review,* 5–12.

20. Cole, "Justice: retributive or reformatitive?" *The Reformed Theological Review,* 5–12.

21. James, "Divine justice and the retributive duty of civil government." *Trinity Journal,* 199–210.

still committed. The state legislation constantly has to review and reconsider sentencing guidelines. And such a retributive approach creates prisons that are overpopulated at unsafe levels. Alabama's retributive justice as a means to deter crime is not working.

OBJECTIVES AND INITIATIVES

Traditional prison ministry in Alabama has its focus in on someone's individual salvation or conversion reflects this retributive view of justice. This approach is limited by its retributive focus. An alternative is to see each person, who has committed a crime as part of a larger system. Drawing on the social gospel, this alternative recognizes that not only does an offender need restoration and reformation, but the entire social system needs to be reformed. Furthermore, the social systems should be participants in the restoration.

This book will utilize restorative justice and the social gospel in order to attempt to strike a balance between an offender's responsibility for his or her offense to the victims, his or herself, and the social system and the need for the system to participate and be involved with a person's restoration back into society. The social gospel not only addresses the individual but the entire social order. It considers all of Jesus' teachings, not just his death, burial, and resurrection. Notwithstanding, the social gospel and restorative justice challenges the offender to consider how his or her actions affected the entire system.

I address and contrast these two different approaches of prison ministry; the traditional approach that aligns with an individualistic gospel and retributive justice against a restorative approach that aligns the social gospel and restorative justice utilizing systems theory. This work will utilize "Family systems process theory" to expand and address self-differentiation and individual responsibility, as well as emotional intelligence. I hope to give the bigger picture of the entire system, how the systems always works to remain balanced, this phenomenon is called, homeostasis, and its discourse, and how restoration works within it or against it.

Finally, I will use systems process theory to create a picture of all the systems working, and how God is working, forgiving, and redeeming through all of life to create a better system in each of our lives, and this world, including someone who was convicted of a crime.

Systems theory talks about "self-differentiation" levels. These scales are considered part of emotional intelligence. Those on the lower scales do not function well in high anxiety situations. Often there is a great deal of dysfunction in the family and inability to think and act clearly. Instead, people will often react to stimuli, even if the action is not in his or her best interest. It is the hope that this project will help people gain higher levels of self-differentiation so he or she can be more aware of high anxiety situations. Unfortunately, people leaving incarceration will face a great deal of high anxiety situations. Some of these situations have already been mentioned, but others will come from people closest to him or her. These situations will come from his or her family. Self-differentiation recognizes the system is always adapting and shifting. However, recognizing sabotage and understanding how each action creates a response will reduce unhealthy thinking and dysfunctional criminal behavior.

Families or the system will sabotage to maintain a level of "homeostasis." When someone transitions out of prison it puts the whole system out of balance, challenging its homeostasis. The system has to adjust. Sabotage can be done by the individual, or done by the system all to return to previous homeostasis. All this creates social problems. These social problems can create high levels of anxiety for someone leaving prison. Anxiety, in this context, will be defined as "the response of an organism to a threat, real or imagined. It is a process that, in some form, is present in all living things."[22] For people transitioning out of prison, the response to high levels of anxiety is to reoffend. Traditional prison ministry's limited focus on conversion only does not engage with the inmate's social system. It fails to recognize that the system was thrown out of balance. Therefore, the entire system has to work through restoration. This is a process. I will introduce this process and help

22. Kerr, and Bowen, *Family Evaluation*, 112.

people recognize the effort and time, which is a lifetime endeavor, to understand how their decisions are part of how the system functions and reacts.

Lastly, systems theory hopes to help the entire system function better. If a person has higher levels of self-differentiation, and is functioning at lower levels of dysfunction, the system will adapt in positive ways. This is where a social gospel approach can utilize God's teachings and seeks to make the world a better place. God is always redeeming and forgiving people. However, when someone positively affects society, it is a picture of God's redemption. When the system forgives a criminal for his or her wrong doing, it is a reflection of God's forgiveness. If normally dysfunctioning systems are adapting and functioning in healthy ways, the world becomes a better place. If someone leaving incarceration understands his or her self and is able to understand the processes within a social system, he or she can improve his or her life. This is the good news of the Gospel. We are called to have life and life more abundantly. (John 10:10, paraphrase mine) People not returning to prison gives life, and life more abundantly.

CONCLUSION

Alabama prisons are overpopulated. Unfortunately, people who leave the ADOC return more often than not. Traditional prison ministries, in Alabama, are so focused on individual salvation that it neglects the whole person. These ministries fail to address the entire social system. Instead, they remain focused on retributive justice and how these people need saving from God's damnation. Then when people return to society, they are osticized and categorized as the socially damned.

Traditional prison ministries teach a gospel that holds anyone has the ability to transcend their past mistakes. But, where is hope when the world is not interested in restoration? What hope is there when everything is placed on the backs of the individual? Where is hope when you don't make enough money to survive? Peter Gomes tells us, "If we want to know how hope works, we must look first to those who suffer, for it is only in and through suffering that hope is made manifest."[23] I propose a communal pastoral care approach that utilizes the social gospel, addresses the social system, and restores the individual offender, sharing a social gospel. A gospel that can be useful to someone leaving prison.

23. Gomes, *The scandalous Gospel of Jesus* 221.

CHAPTER 2

Prison Ministry Theology

BACKGROUND

Reevaluation of Prison Ministry

TRADITIONAL PRISON MINISTRY, IN its most common form, is very individualistic. Typically, traditional prison ministry has had one common pedagogy, share the gospel for individual conversion. Its ordinary focus or theology is what is considered the "Jesus only" model. This model follows a misinterpretation of a central passage in Matthew. The interpretation explains that Jesus told his listeners that when they visited a prisoner, they were, in fact, visiting Jesus himself. (Matthew 25: 31–46). Yet, instead of seeing Jesus in the prisoner, this interpretation sees the prisoner in need of Jesus. This basis is the most general foundation to begin traditional prison ministry because those in prison, even if this was their own doing, need visiting. They need people who show they care and need the gospel shared to them. Therefore, traditional prison ministry, to-day, is limited to saving the individual sinner from Hell and eternal damnation.

Yet, this is often where traditional prison ministry fails or at least is in need of expansion because it falls short or misses the mark. It neglects the social system, the aftercare, discipleship, or pastoral care component. "Jesus only" prison ministry is only focused on getting the individual sinner saved. Its core focus is on the individual and neglects the family and social conditions. It neglects that how we treat the prisoner is how we treat Jesus. Furthermore, this type of prison ministry, while building the person up while in prison, neglects care for those who eventually leave prison. It follows an individual clinical approach to pastoral care.

However, pastoral care is shifting away from this individual approach known as the clinical approach. Nancy Ramsay states, "'Sea change' is a phrase that characterizes the dramatic changes in pastoral care, counseling, and pastoral theology since the publication of the *Dictionary of Pastoral Care and Counseling* (1990)"[1] There is more taken into consideration now. There is a broader perspective that considers the different needs based on interplay of social structures. Ramsay explains,

> ". . . that two new paradigms have emerged that are gradually eclipsing the Clinical Pastoral Paradigm. The Communal Contextual and the Intercultural Paradigms reflect the significant intellectual, cultural, political, and religious dynamics that characterized the end of the twentieth century and continue early in the twenty-first Century." [2]

I would argue this broader perspective needs to create an alternative to traditional prison ministry. Prisons are filling up at a record pace, and most of the people in the criminal justice system will filter in and out of prison. However, what obstacles will these people transitioning out of prison face? Traditional prison ministry has not really addressed this. The individual model of prison ministry is not effective. Further, it reflects a truncated individualized gospel in which pastoral care is not provided to the family and the transitioning inmate. Therefore, I wish to contrast aspects of the individual model of traditional prison ministry to a restorative, communal, systems model of prison ministry. This

1. Ramsay, N. J. *Pastoral care and counseling,* 1.

2. Ramsay, N. J. *Pastoral care and counseling,* 1.

contrast will focus on four areas: the gospel, restorative justice, sin and pastoral care.

The Gospel to prisoners?

What is the Gospel? "Jesus saves" is such a common message, especially in traditional prison ministry. But what does that mean for someone previously incarcerated? Where is Jesus when it seems like society is completely against you? Where is God when the bills are not paid? Where is God when the probation or parole officer makes you wait for an hour during monthly/weekly report-in? Where is Jesus when finances are overwhelming, but only places paying menial wages offer employment to felons? Does Jesus really save someone from all the troubles a previously incarcerated individual faces? "What is the gospel in these dilemmas? Not, what do we do, but what does the gospel mean here?"[3] Many prison ministries tell people to give all to God and God will take care of everything. However, many people transitioning out of prison feel as if God has abandoned them. This is certainly the case in Alabama. Traditional prison ministries, churches, and other organizations focus on the individual who committed the crime and not the whole system. The church and traditional prison ministries talk about redemption, but what does it mean to be redeemed? What about those who feel they are beyond redemption? How does someone exiting the ADOC and traditional prison ministry experience God's redemption in a society that is not interested in his or her redemption?

A first step to contrast traditional prison ministry and a restorative prison ministry on redemption requires addressing the concept of God. The concept of God is shaped by social constructs. Even if the social construct begins with a simple idea, that idea can shape a person's view of God. Unfortunately, the simple idea of God among felons, with traditional prison ministry, is rejection. Alabama disenfranchises a person once he or she is convicted of

---

3. Stone and Duke, *How to think theologically*, 66.

a crime. Until recently, a person with a drug felony was not able to receive food assistance. Until recently, a voting commission determined if a crime was one of moral turpitude, and the same commission could take away someone's right to vote. Now there is a specific list of crimes that remove someone's ability to vote. Most licensing boards in Alabama will not consider someone who has ever had a felony conviction. Traditional prison ministries in Alabama focus on how bad an individual is a sinner and how much the individual needs God's grace and forgiveness. The general view of God in traditional prison ministry is rejection, not love and redemption, and lacks seeing Jesus in the prisoner.

Traditional prison ministries have to improve on their ability to help people experience the love and redemption of God or else address the questions as to why God is ignoring these people in their plight. These ministries must become a safe place for people of all walks to come and work out salvation. In Alabama, traditional prison ministries are multi-denominational, the primary focus is on individual Christian conversion while incarcerated. These various prison ministries do not offer much to an incarcerated individual transition back into society. The larger church is not doing much better in prison transition ministry representing grace and redemption. Bob Ekblad states,

> "One of the greatest barriers between mainstream Christians and people on the margins is that mainstream Christians often represent the dominant culture and do little to nothing to distinguish themselves from it. Few Christians would deny the importance of communicating grace, unconditional love and forgiveness of sin in Jesus Christ. Yet the church is often silent about issues that directly affect the poor."[4]

This individualized punishment focused traditional prison ministry is unsatisfactory, it does not see Jesus in the prisoner, it lacks Christian compassion, and is not finally redemptive.

---

4. Ekblad, *Reading the Bible with the Damned*, xvi.

Restorative Justice

A restorative prison ministry will work to reveal grace, redemption, compassion, and to restore these formerly incarcerated persons to full life in the community. This reflects a restorative justice approach. Pfeil explains, "Restorative justice affords people the opportunity to identify and commit to key values, e.g., fostering human dignity, procedural equity, personal and communal accountability, and inclusive participation."[5] Prisons and traditional prison ministry focused on retributive justice, are about demeaning and humiliating a person. People are caged and often treated like an animal. This treatment is meant to take away someone's humanity. It reflects not seeing Jesus in the prisoner. Thus, once someone returns to society, people continue to reject them for their past mistakes, or their institutional survival behavior. Unfortunately, this does leave many options for someone transitioning out of prison. After so much rejection, people often reoffend and return.

This behavior is connected with feeling that they are beyond redemption. They do not see themselves as created by God and redeemed by Jesus. A restorative prison ministry should work to change this thinking utilizing the social gospel and a restorative justice approach. Restorative justice works to make a better society and reduce recidivism. Amy Levad, in an article concerning restorative justice, writes, "Studies revealing the effectiveness of some restorative justice programs in reducing recidivism rates and empowering people to return to their communities as healthy and functional neighbors and citizens suggest that this turn to restorative justice is well founded in criminological evidence."[6] The purpose of restorative justice is not only to reduce recidivism, but also to address the needs of victims and to re-establish communal norms of behavior and relationship, among other things. "Common good is undermined by criminal behavior; it is also

5. Pfeil, "A theological understanding of restorative justice" 159.

6. Levad, "Restorative and transformative justice in a land of mass incarceration," 23.

undermined by giving up on those that have broken the law."[7] Therefore, a restorative prison ministry needs to fully embrace a program of restorative justice that restores the offender and recognizes the victim as both are affected by the crime event.

Crime, Sin and the gospel

The crime event is complex. This complexity puts prison ministry in a complicated position. It must address the need for justice for the victims of crimes. The victims have been hurt and care must be provided. However, the Christian message is also one of grace and forgiveness for the person who committed the crime. Yet, traditional prison ministry has focused on the need for repentance based on individual failure and punishment leaving it difficult for someone previously incarcerated to experience redemption and grace. Michelle Alexander writes, "In church, families of prisoners often keep secret the imprisonment of their children or relatives. Churches can be a place where judgment, shame, and contempt are felt most acutely."[8] Part of the care that needs to be offered to people released from prison is a sound theology concerning guilt, sin, and redemption. However, these theological terms must be fleshed out with the church or ministry to move beyond individualistic conceptions.

Sin is addressed either in traditional focus on individual moral failure or a view in which sin is more involved than simply breaking the law or wrongdoing. Mark Biddle explains, "For most people, the very term sin evokes images of the moralist listing and decrying specific actions. However, this sin as crime or event, which is part truth does not provide the full biblical witness to what sin is and the problems within. The dynamics of sin (like crime) in everyday life are far more complex."[9] Understanding these complexities and recognizing the wrongdoing is necessary for any person,

7. Levad, "'I was in prison and you visited me': a sacramental approach to rehabilitative and restorative criminal justice," 93–11.2.

8. Alexander, *The New Jim Crow*, 166.

9. Biddle, *Missing the mark*, xii+.

much less someone who has broken the law. "A sturdy Christian doctrine of sin allows us to hold truths together, acknowledging that we are children of God who are also deeply fallen."[10]

However, sin in the restorative approach to prison ministry, does more than remind us that we are flawed beings. The crimes and victims should convict us but grace is available. There exists a legal prejudice against people who have been convicted of breaking the law and traditional prison reflects that prejudice with its individual focus. However, prison ministries and churches should practice a redemption that reflects a social theology and a social gospel that attends to more than individual moral failure.

The Bible challenges us all to think, work and believe far beyond ourselves. We are a social people, with a nature to commune together. The Apostle Paul in Romans tells us, "we, who are many, are one Body" (Romans 12:5, NRSV) and again makes reference to a body having many parts but still one body (1 Corinthians 12:12–27, NRSV). It seems to be a common message of the Apostle Paul referencing inclusion of the Gentile people in Ephecians 3:6, making one body. However, if Paul's words are not enough we can consider the writer of 1 John who writes, "we have fellowship with one another, and the blood of Jesus, his Son, purifies us from all sin." (1 John 1:7, NRSV) Therein lies a problem with the individual gospel, the Bible challenges us to work in community as one body. Rauschenbusch writes, "The individualistic gospel has taught us to see the sinfulness of every human heart. But it has not given us an adequate understanding of the sinfulness of the social order and its share in the sins of all individuals within it."[11]

A major argument made traditionally against the social gospel has been about its view of sin. "Its teachings seem to put the blame for wrongdoing on the environment, and instead of stiffening and awakening the sense of responsibility in the individual, it teaches him or her to unload it on society."[12] I will argue that this is an erroneous view of the social gospel and sin.

10. Craigo-Snell, and Monroe, *Living Christianity*, 93.
11. Rauschenbusch, *A Theology for the Social Gospel*, 5.
12. Rauschenbusch, *A Theology for the Social Gospel*, 32–33.

A restorative view, drawing from the social gospel, of sin will stand apart from the traditional watered-down cliché that says, "If you talk right, speak right, or act right then everything will be alright." Instead, a restorative view of sin will recognize failure and the need for transforming grace. For a ministry or church to help someone recognize the sin committed and hurt caused can create resistance. However, the benefits of understanding the effects of sin will help understand the need for God. This will help people recognize failure and strengthen their need for grace. This sin/grace complexity that is both social and individual has yet to be addressed in traditional prison ministries. The gospel, in its full view of redemption, demands a more social and less individualistic view of sin, grace, and redemption.

The gospel is reflected differently. "Coming to an understanding of the gospel's meaning (in traditional v restorative prison ministry) is a bottom-line issue for every Christian. Have we received any good news we can count on? How are we to describe the effects and benefits of the gospel message?"[13] These are valid questions to consider with the "Jesus only" or conversion focused traditional prison ministry. Will the gospel shared have a lasting effect besides avoiding an eternal Hell after death? Can we develop a restorative prison ministry that cares about the Hell people will face leaving prison? Using the social gospel, a restorative prison ministry, seeks to address these special questions. In traditional prison ministry the individual gospel reveals a strong sense of individual sin and the need for individual grace but neglects social redemption.

The social gospel does consider social redemption. "The social gospel is the old message of salvation, but enlarged and intensified."[14] The church and prison ministries need to embody this enlarged and intensified gospel. The social gospel focuses on the kingdom of God. Jesus' primary message was on the kingdom of God and the coming age. He modeled a prayer saying, "Your kingdom come, your will be done, on earth as it is in heaven." (Matthew 6:10, NRSV) "Social gospel adherents understand that

13. Stone and Duke, *How to think theologically*, 69.
14. Rauschenbusch, *A Theology for the Social Gospel*, 5.

the 'kingdom of God' is not some faraway and/or theoretical eschatological enterprise located either in heaven or at the end of the age; it was something to be brought into being in this world by the application of Christian principles to the least in society."[15] What good is it to preach to and convert individual prisoners if nothing is done to help them function better in society? The gospel, the social gospel calls, compels and challenges us to create a restorative prison ministry that will address social conditions. This will involve more than simply saving someone's individual wretched soul from eternal damnation. Restorative prison ministry calls for both individual change, and attention to social relations as part of that change.

CONTEXT

Pastoral Care and Systems Theory

How can a church or ministry do more than individual "conversion only" prison ministry? How can it practice restorative justice that cares for both victims and offenders? How can it move beyond individual care to social care? The individual or clinical model type of pastoral care has dominated much of prison ministry. It is focused primarily on the inmate and his or her crime. Pastoral care, as already mentioned, is experiencing a paradigm shift. Prison ministry must consider these shifts as well.

A new approach to pastoral care is the communal contextual paradigm. "The communal contextual paradigm includes ecclesial communities of care and the importance of cultural and political contexts shaping persons' lives."[16] These contexts carry considerable weight in how a person functions. Systems theory reflects the communal contextual model because it considers how systems function and gives a broad view of causes, effects, and anxiety. Systems theory "focuses less on content and more on the process that

---

15. Gomes, *The scandalous Gospel of Jesus,* 165.
16. Ramsay, N. J. *Pastoral care and counseling,* 11.

governs."[17] Systems theory moves beyond an individual and his or her problem and considers the whole social system. The idea is to address the process behind the functioning, not just the particular action. However, there are quite a few challenges walking someone through the web of their family system and discovering dysfunction. Those challenges reflect the five basic concepts of the family model. "These concepts are self-differentiation, identified patient, homeostasis, extended family field, and emotional triangles."[18]

System theory uses the term "self-differentiation" which recognizes the emotional pulls and processes in a family but remains non-anxious. Self-differentiation is a process. "The process becomes a lifelong project for most people who begin it and it often follows several predictable steps that are repeated over and over again."[19] While the clinical model of pastoral care addresses the self, systems theory addresses boundaries and protection of self. "Differentiation means the capacity of a family member to define his or her own life's goals and values apart from surrounding togetherness pressures. It includes the capacity to maintain a (relatively) non-anxious presence in the midst of anxious systems."[20] Some of the aforementioned challenges previously incarcerated inmates face can be addressed by helping them move to higher scales of self-differentiation. "Well-differentiated people are able to be themselves, to do and say what they want, think, and feel without undue concern about whether others will like them or criticize them, and without a need to either flatter or criticize others inappropriately."[21] Attempting to walk someone from dysfunction and incarceration to becoming a self-differentiated, well functioning member of society has tremendous challenges. The person needs to have a sound understanding of his or her self and his or her redemption as involving more than individual conversion. Unfortunately, society is not interested in her or her redemption

17. Friedman, *Generation to generation*, 15.
18. Friedman, *Generation to generation*, 15–19.
19. Gilbert, *Extraordinary relationships*, 121.
20. Friedman, *Generation to generation*, 27.
21. Richardson, *Family ties that bind*, 36.

and will likely sabotage attempts to move forward. "Once a person is labeled a felon, he or she is ushered into a parallel universe in which discrimination, stigma, and exclusion are perfectly legal, and privileges of citizenship such as voting and jury service are off-limits. It is a badge of inferiority. For those released on probation or parole, the risks are especially high."[22] Therefore, helping a previously incarcerated person understand and achieve higher levels of self-differentiation is vital for a post-prison ministry that draws from the integration of the social gospel and systems theory.

People coming out of prison are considered the problem in traditional prison ministry. Once a person has been convicted of a crime it is easy with a retributive focus to shift blame to that person. This is called the identified patient. "The concept of the identified patient is that the family member with the obvious symptom is to be seen not as the 'sick one' but as the one in whom the family's stress or pathology has surfaced."[23] It is easy in a retributive focus for previously incarcerated individuals to fall into the category as the identified patient. This person creates immense amounts of anxiety. Will the person re-offend? How much will this person interrupt regular everyday life? How much money has the person cost the family? Incarceration simply creates stress and the justice system does not help people get back on their feet. Therefore, a retributive system isolates this person as, "the problem."

However, in systems theory "the purpose of using the phrase identified patient is to avoid isolating the 'problemed family member from the overall relationship system of the family."[24] "Each family member develops a unique personality, but not in a vacuum. Each personality is developed in relation and response to the other personalities in the family."[25] This goes beyond family systems into the social system. Criminals freed into society are not afforded many rights, and the prejudices against them are great. "They are entitled to no respect and little moral concern, criminals

22. Alexander, *The New Jim Crow*, 94.

23. Friedman, *Generation to generation*, 19.

24. Friedman, *Generation to generation*, 20.

25. Richardson, *Family ties that bind*, 8.

today are deemed a characterless and purposeless people, deserving of our collective scorn and contempt."[26] It is quite difficult for the previously incarcerated individual to move beyond being the identified patient that creates anxiety to the family and social structures around them. However, restorative prison ministries can help the previously incarcerated individual shift and change how he or she responds to the system which will likely affect and possibly change the system itself.

Change is hard for most people. In families, this is especially true. Each family system works or functions in a way that creates a balance. However, if that balance is ever interrupted, the system works to self-correct. This concept is known as homeostasis. "Every time a family member gets in trouble with the law, does well academically, gets a promotion, has a baby or is hospitalized, the rest of the family compensates. This compensation happens whether the original change is good or bad."[27] When someone breaks the law and becomes incarcerated, the family, as mentioned, compensates. It creates a system of function or over-functioning to deal with the absence of the incarcerated individual. What happens when he or she returns? "One phenomena of the power of homeostasis is that whenever a (person) attempts to bring about change he or she will most certainly encounter sabotage."[28] The same is true in society. However, in restorative prison ministry recognizing the power and difference and working within these powers allows someone to function and withstand the sabotage and help everyone function better. This, unfortunately, is easier said than done. Yet it is possible for someone to get out of prison and become a functioning member of society. It will be hard and society will push against it, but it is possible. It is more complicated when considering the struggles within the family and recognizing the sabotaging that exists simply to resist change. However, understanding this principle "elucidates the resistance families have to change."[29]

26. Alexander, *The New Jim Crow*, 141.
27. Richardson, *Family ties that bind*, 9.
28. Galindo, *Perspectives on congregational leadership*, 31.
29. Friedman, *Generation to generation*, 24.

Who makes up the family system? Where does society fit in the system? What system will a person coming out of prison need to understand and consider? "The only members of the extended family that the (classical model of pastoral care) tends to consider important are one's parents and their influence . . . . In contrast, family theory sees the entire network of the extended family as important and the influence of that network is considered to be significant in the here and now as well."[30] Understanding the entire family or seeing the entire system helps someone understand all the processes at work. It helps someone see anxiety at play given different situations. "The notion of social identity or social location is a crucial concept for any discussion of power, difference, and postmodernity."[31] These positions dictate and form functioning patterns and reveal symptoms of anxiety. "Our position in our extended families affects how we function in other relationships. . ."[32] Societal power works against previously incarcerated individuals. As mentioned, rights are taken away, the ability to work in a job with a decent wage, and it creates a power struggle. The extended family in anyone's system reveals how the family functions within the system and works the power struggles. "Every family and every relationship has rules. Families develop many different spoken and unspoken rules on how to function."[33] Society has done the same. Extended family recognizes how functioning works within these struggles.

Families, and society systems are made up of relationships. A dynamic of these relationships is a relationship triangle. "A triangle is any three-way relationship."[34] The most common in a family is that of dad, mom, and child. Moreover, love triangles consist of a husband, wife, mister/mistress. For people coming out of prison, the justice triangle consists of criminal, system, and victim. "Triangles are not good or bad they are merely the

30. Friedman, *Generation to generation,* 24.

31. Ramsay, *Pastoral care and counseling,* 66.

32. Friedman, *Generation to Generation,* 295.

33. Galindo, *Perspectives on congregational leadership,* 25.

34. Richardson, *Family ties that bind,* 51.

product of emotional process and anxiety."[35] "Triangles connect to each other through a series of interlocks to the members of the extended family or system."[36] Triangles simply exist. When the relationship between two people gets too intense, it is easier to take the pressure off by involving someone else. However, this creates problems of over-functioning and under-functioning. Sometimes, a corner of the triangle is not a person, but an object or an addiction. Often incarcerations and criminal behavior stem from drug usage. The family has to compensate for someone's drug use by over-functioning. This gives the incarcerated individual the ability to under-function. There are a lot of dynamics at play. However, it is vital for a person to understand the processes and functioning that interlocks these triangles.

Methodology

I want to create a restorative prison ministry that draws upon systems theory and the social gospel to minister to transitioning inmates back into society. This research will be limited to eight former inmates paroled out of prison. It will also be limited to Alabama.[37] Alabama has people who are considered high risk parole. These men and women have a history of recidivism. This context will be the primary focus of this project. This research will not involve sex offenders. There is a great need; however, there is a far more complex problem and the aforementioned challenges are heightened to registered sex offenders. Much of the work will be ethnographic and so it will involve observation and focus group interviews. "A key element of almost every ethnographic research project, participant observation might also be described as 'going to see for oneself.'[38]

35. Galindo, *Perspectives on congregational leadership*, 25.

36. Gilbert, *Extraordinary relationships*, 77.

37. I do not address the known issues of race in regards to mass incarceration and unjust sentencing. I am a white male of a certain privilege which would make addressing these concerns either anecdotal or unrealistic.

38. Moschella, *Ethnography as a pastoral practice*, 233.

The first step, in the restorative prison ministry, is to walk the person(s) through drawing a genogram. I used Reagan, Bloomer, and Galindo's *A Family Genogram workbook.* This book allows the person to see the complexity of the family system and some of the emotional dynamics already at play. The genogram lets the person be an expert in his or her family. It shows how homeostasis exists, interlocking triangles, and distance and closeness of various relationships. Hopefully, each person will gain a higher level of self-differentiation. Moreover, the person will be able to resist the social and family sabotage and ultimately recognize and understand sin and the redemption and grace that God has provided.

I attempted to have each participant read and discuss Ronald Richardson's book *Becoming Your Best.* I wanted it to serve as a guidebook through the journey these men or women will take and introduce systems theory. After each meeting, I challenged them to apply some of the concepts that would allow him or her to be better self differentiated and notice the resistance within the system. These meetings were held in focus group style, where these people can share their stories, challenges, and enlighten me to new challenges I had not considered. It is my hope that this will grow into a transitional ministry that allows people to see how sin affects his or her life, experience God's grace and redemption, and understand the systems in place and how they affect the functioning in his or her life.

Unfortunately, systems theory is a lifetime learning endeavor. It is never ending work. This ministry project was limited to a 3 months of study. Therefore qualitative results will be utilized. This ministry will help released persons to uncover certain dysfunctional behavior. This restorative ministry project will show how all the relationships tangle and interconnect. These interconnected relationships are affected by each others actions, and each situation causes a reaction. This restorative prison ministry seeks to give a picture and provide tools for a person leaving prison to understand his or her offenses and how it affected the entire system. This work wishes to challenge the formerly incarcerated to recognize their triggers, or provoke a certain reaction. It hopes to help them resist these provocations. While this ministry will hold that formerly incarcerated persons are responsible and able to change themselves, but also that each action can affect the whole system, good and bad. Therefore, this restorative prison ministry wishes to measure emotional maturity. It wishes to measure improvements in relationships and a person's overall function in a societal system.

Qualitative results are difficult to measure. However, this ministry project will utilize focus group interviews. The results will be measured using qualitative data. Christian Scharen explains, "Some researchers find qualitative methods too narrow and its findings too anecdotal to be of any real scientific value."[39] He goes on to explain that other "scientists use qualitative methods and find substantial value in them."[40] Verbatims will be the primary tool for theological reflection and learning. These verbatims will give me qualitative data revealing either better functioning within the larger system, or continued dysfunction.

CONCLUSION

People leaving incarceration face tremendous challenges. Many are struggling with debts, drug addictions, family issues, children issues, housing issues. Each situation is different. These diverse settings need to direct traditional prison ministries away from a "cookie cutter" way of doing ministry. Instead, these differing situations call for a more complex approach to prison ministry than the individual "Jesus only" approach. These different social settings call for a social gospel. The social gospel addresses the complexities of sin, and the need for justification, and redemption for the individual and the social system. I wanted to learn about the social context of formerly incarcerated persons. Utilizing the contextual cultural model of pastoral care, ethnographic research is required. When providing pastoral care to these prisoners or previously incarcerated people, I address their current levels of

39. Scharen, and Vigen, *Ethnography as Christian theology*, 5.
40. Scharen and Vigen, *Ethnography as Christian theology*, 5.

functioning, and find out their particular situation. Ethnography allows them to be the expert in their situation. They are allowed to provide no wrong answers but simply give their story. Scharen and Vigen explain, "Human relationships are at the heart of pastoral ethnography."[41] Ethnography allows the researcher the ability to walk with these inmates and understand their struggles and offer pastoral care, as God walks with each of us in our struggles.

People who have been convicted of a crime have a hard time seeing that God still cares. Society often does not. However, the greatness of the "social gospel is the clearness and insistence with which it sets forth the necessity and the possibility of redeeming the historical life of humanity from the social wrongs which now pervade it."[42] It allows people to see that God still loves them. "This does not mean that God's love is blind. God sees us as we really are."[43] Yet, God still redeems us all. Understanding God's redemption is necessary when doing family of origin work because sometimes the family does not forgive. The job market can be unforgiving. Everything surrounding someone coming out of prison can be quite unforgiving. Hopefully, each person will gain a higher level of self-differentiation. Moreover, the person will be able to resist the social and family sabotage and ultimately recognize and understand his or her sin and redemption that God has provided. Hopefully, each previously incarcerated individual will be able to see and experience God in a new way.

Prison ministry is challenging. Prisons are filled with people who deserve to be incarcerated. Some of these people have done terrible things. Yet God still loves these people and created him or her in God's image. Most of these people will get out and be returned to society. Restorative prison ministry is necessary to help people function better in a society that is not interested in redemption for prisoners. Focusing on the specific crime event, or bad behavior can be limiting because it focuses on the symptom and does not consider the social relations. Understanding

41. Scharen and Vigen, *Ethnography as Christian theology,* 86.

42. Rauschenbusch, *A Theology for the Social Gospel,* 95.

43. Guthrie, *Christian Doctrine,* 319.

the social relations and how they relate to the overall system is a lifetime endeavor. The work is hard. The person will sometimes fail and return to his or her previous behavior. Some simply will not get it. However, God calls us to do the difficult work of sharing the gospel, the social gospel. I am reminded of a litany I read, it states,

> "We trust in God: who sits down in our midst to share our humanity; who takes us beyond safe places into action, vulnerability, and into the streets; and challenges us to work for change, to bear responsibility, to take risks, to stand with those on the margins, and be used by the Spirit to build communities of hope."[44]

Prison ministry calls those who endeavor to be involved to take risks and stand with those on the margins and with the Spirit's empowering, build communities of hope.

---

44. Taken from a worship guide at Weatherly Heights Baptist church, Huntsville, AL adapted from Iona community Iona Abbey Worship Book.

CHAPTER 3

A Restorative Prison Ministry

IN THIS CHAPTER I will provide information about the participants who have transitioned out of prison, the meetings where the meetings took place, the topics of instruction, and edited verbatims showing the process of Systems Theory work. I will also present the goals, objectives and initiatives implemented along with the process for communal contextual pastoral care project. I will provide a clear definition of the social gospel and how it differs from the individual gospel, the theology behind both retributive justice and restorative justice and some lesson topics and techniques used in studying and providing care for these people transitioning out of prison. Finally, I will review the results of the focus group and the systems work done that are part of this project.

PARTICIPANTS

The participants of this project came from a variety of settings. Some were from personal relationships with the researcher. Others came from the "Daily Reporting Center" (DRC). However, each participant agreed to engage in this ethnographic study. Moreover, each participant agreed to the identifier as Participant and initials of their name, i.e.Participant B, for both privacy and protection of their reputation.

Participant A is a married man with two kids. He was convicted of possession of a controlled substance, and has been arrested for other charges but not convicted. Participant A is currently on parole from a 10 year sentence. He works in the construction business on crews framing houses.

Participant C is an unmarried man without kids. However, he lives with his mother, step-dad, and 2 of 3 siblings. Participant C was convicted of multiple possession of a controlled substance charges. Participant C has been unemployed for about a year.

Participant T is a divorced woman with one child. She is currently homeless, living in a hotel. She was convicted of possession of a controlled substance. She served a 36 month sentence, but was released early on what is known as "good time."[1] Participant T lost custody of her child, and is unemployed.

Participant J is a divorced woman with four children. J lives with friends and has not had custody of her children for several years. She is currently unemployed and continues to struggle with her addiction. Participant J served 1 year in prison before being released on parole.

Participant S is an unmarried woman without kids. She was convicted of various drug charges and served a 4 year prison sentence. She lives in an apartment with her boyfriend and another roommate. Participant S is employed working in fast food retail.

Participant R is a divorced man with two children. He currently lives with his ex-wife but not in the interest of reconciliation. He was recently released from prison on parole from a 15 year sentence for multiple theft and burglary charges. He has been to prison 3 times in the past. Participant R is unemployed.

Participant K is an unmarried man with one child. He lives with his child. He was convicted of theft of property related to an automobile. He completed a 2 year prison sentence and has

---

1. A person with lower offenses can qualify for a deduction from his or her term up to seventy-five days for every 30 days served.

reoffended but with smaller theft charges. Participant K is employed as a delivery driver.

Participant B is a widowed man with 5 grown step children. He lives on his own and works in the auto industry. He was convicted of multiple theft charges and served prison sentences in multiple states including Alabama.

The group is made up of 5 men and 3 women. There was an equal divide of black and white participants. The ages ranged from as high as 62 to 26. Each participant had some involvement in the christian church and was involved in some sort of Christian prison ministry during their time with the ADOC.

GOALS AND OBJECTIVES

The goal of this project was to create an awareness of how each person transitioning out of prison is part of a system that is larger than his or herself. It seeks to address how sin and crime affect the entire system. The project seeks to challenge the participants to recognize the dysfunction within that system and function within it.

The hypothesis of this project is that recidivism is both a system problem and a personal challenge. People transitioning out of prison are not equipped to understand how a family or social system adapts and works to maintain a balance or homeostasis. Therefore, any change, both good and bad, the system will adapt, adjust, and in some cases sabotage. Unfortunately, a person transitioning out of prison will most likely face a great deal of sabotage. Notwithstanding, if he or she has a better understanding of emotional process and a higher level of self-differentiation, he or she can withstand that sabotage and function within society. The system will then adjust and adapt to the new normal.

APPLICATION

The participants met with me at a local coffee shop. They have a cozy meeting space that provides privacy and a casual relaxed atmosphere. We agreed to meet two times a week for three months. We would meet on Monday and Wednesdays for the next several weeks. Unfortunately, as the project progressed, some participants did withdraw without notice. Each participant had the opportunity to discuss their progress and struggles working through their family and social influences. Also addressing sin and the crime dynamic. integrating back into society. The outline of the material presented was as follows: an introduction to the family and social system, anxiety and family behavior, homeostasis and forgiveness, understanding self and self-differentiation, sabotage and triangles and how to function within dysfunction. Each of these themes created conversation about several other such as the crime/sin dynamic, emotional processes, and restorative justice.

INTRODUCTION TO THE FAMILY/SOCIAL SYSTEM

The beginning discussion centered around how we are made up of something bigger than ourselves. When someone commits a crime and is incarcerated for that crime, it affects both the individual and the family and society of that individual. In like manner, when a person exits incarceration and re-enters society, it affects both the individual and the family and society surroundings. "Not only does family affect the development, behavior, and well-being of its individual members, so too does each individual member affect the family's development, behavior, and well-being."[2] Newton's third law of physics states that every action (good or bad) creates an equal or greater reaction.[3] This same principle applies to families. This discussion will center around two topics. What happens when the system is wronged? What is the emotional process of forgiveness?

2. Stojkovic, *Prisoner reentry,* 88.

3. Newton's Third Law.

Anxiety and Family behavior

I opened with a question about the participants' family behavior. I asked if anyone ever noticed how things within your own family gets shaken up when change occurs? How did your family react when you were arrested? Participant C began the discussion saying, "My family did not seem to care. It was just part of it. Almost everyone in my family had an arrest record so no one seemed to make a big deal." I pressed his response asking, if it is possible you just did not notice? Even if families expect something to happen such as people getting arrested, they still compensate for the change. "Yea, I guess they did, they just didn't seem to care." Participant A said, "My wife was my girlfriend at the time, she was rather upset at me. I think she had intentions of leaving me at first. Obviously, I am glad she didn't. My mom was the one who really was affected." How so? "She put money she didn't have on my books, and paid for me a lawyer. She didn't have the money to pay the power bill but yet she was putting money towards me. Thinking back on it, I am not sure how I feel about it." Would you say she was making reckless decisions financially? "Definitely, but she does that when something is wrong she attempts to fix it but it is almost always to her detriment." Participant T said, "My family did similar. My mother and step-father owned their own business that they borrowed money against it to pay my bond and attorney's fee." Did anyone else's family sacrifice a great deal financially once arrested? (All but 2 raised their hands)

Moving the discussion forward, I asked, what do you think of when you hear the word anxiety? Almost all of you mentioned when you were arrested, your family made some financial sacrifices. How was it when you went to prison? Participant K said, "My mother cried." Participant T said that her mother did as well. Participant R explained, "The first time his family was affected, but when he went back it seemed they got colder and colder toward him." I asked him, "Do you think they were just fed up with you?" "Yeah, there was hope the first time I got out but when I kept going back, they seemed to just accept it." Accept what? "That I will just keep going back." Do you think you will go back again? "Probably." This mentality reflects what Edwin Friedman calls the "Vicious cycle."[4] He explains,

> "Chronic family anxiety (the fear of you being gone to prison) leads to a physical or emotional symptom. (In this case, committing a crime.) The eruption of the symptom, however creates a specific anxiety in response to the symptom. Focus on the illness now deflects the original chronic anxiety. When the identified patient (you) begins to recuperate, the specific anxiety that had been focused on the illness goes down, but the original chronic anxiety (you being gone to prison) if there is no change in the system, will begin to rise again."[5]

I used a notepad to draw out how this vicious cycle works in crime. I explained, your family being afraid of you repeat offending creates anxiety, causing a downward curve of behaviors. You respond to those behaviors by committing a crime. You get arrested and go to prison, confirming the original anxiety. Therefore, when you get out, unless addressed, the cycle begins again. As a follow up question concerning Participant R's discussion, I asked if anyone else experience something like this? Participant A said, "Not about prison but more about drugs." "My wife still thinks I will eventually go back to using drugs." Did you ever notice how your family reacted to you using? "I am sure they had to do a lot of things, I wasn't in a good place." Did they take care of your kids? "Yes, and took care of many other things. I have put my family through it." So her fear is valid? "No, she just worries over nothing, I am not going back to that life."

Closing the session, I asked the participants how well they understood anxiety in terms of family systems theory. I wanted to make sure each understood how their family reacts and responds to high and low anxiety situations. I wanted everyone to recognize how each of them responds and reacts when anxiety is high or low.

---

4. Stojkovic, *Prisoner reentry*, 131.

5. Stojkovic, *Prisoner reentry*, 131.

Homeostasis and Forgiveness

The next session, I wanted to talk about homeostasis in family systems theory and how it relates to sin/crime and forgiveness. I explained that each family is working to compensate for your incarceration. "Family systems, by design, attempt to maintain internal stability, balance, and constancy; in systems terminology, homeostasis is the self-regulating principle of a system preserving its equilibrium."[6] All of you have discussed how their family adjusted and in every case over functioned while you were away in prison. However, have any of you considered how your family had to adjust to you going to and coming out of prison? All families and social systems adjust to change. Unfortunately, when we leave the prison system and go back to our normal life, we want everything to go back to normal. Notwithstanding, the family/social system created a new normal. "The criminal justice system places many demands on individuals and their families over time. Families not only struggle to cope with the family member's incarceration but also with that family member's reentry."[7]

I asked the participants, Does the concept of homeostasis and forgiveness work together? There is a cliche saying to forgive and forget. Theologically, I was taught that God took our sin and cast it in the depths of the sea. (Micah 7:19) However, can God forget? I know I cannot forget what I did. I wanted so bad for an expungement opportunity so that my record could be erased. Unfortunately, nothing can ever erase what I did. My family had to live and adjust to what I did. They had to alter their lives because of my choices. Am I to expect them to forget what they had to go through for my misgivings? When I sinned and committed a crime, I wronged an entire system. My criminal act made the entire system off balance. It had to adjust. I had to work my way through some of that adjustments and how me coming back in the picture created a new adjustment.

---

6. Stojkovic, *Prisoner reentry,* 91.

7. Stojkovic, *Prisoner reentry,* 93.

Considering all the adjustments each of our families had to make, is it fair to expect them to just forgive and forget? Sin and forgiveness are far more complex than what we originally thought. Provoking discussion, I asked, what is your family's emotional process of forgiveness? Participant A: "It is hard for me to tell. I don't think mine has really forgiven me yet." Participant T: "Mine wants to keep me cooped up and protect me like a child from all the evils of drugs. They are so afraid I will relapse." Participant C: "My family has seemingly distanced themselves from me. While I live with them, they make my life a living hell." Have any of you actually asked for forgiveness? Participant S: "Yes, and most of my family did, but it took awhile for them to come around. But, there are still a few in my family that won't have anything to do with me, no matter what I do or don't do." Participant J: "I have told my family I am sorry, but they do not believe me because its like I can't quit messing up."

Does anyone ever feel stuck when attempting to obtain forgiveness? Does it ever feel like you have to try harder, work harder, pay more money, do more, act more, whatever it is more just so that your family, or society will eventually forgive you? (All agreed) Friedman explains, "Conceptually stuck systems cannot become unstuck simply by trying harder. For a fundamental reorientation to occur, a spirit of adventure that optimizes serendipity and enables new perceptions beyond the control of our thinking processes must happen first."[8] Unfortunately, each of us cannot control whether a society, family, or friend ever forgives us. Instead, we can get caught on a treadmill of trying harder attempting to gain this forgiveness. "The treadmill of trying harder is driven by the assumption that failure is due to the fact that one did not try hard enough, use the right technique, or get enough information."[9] Notwithstanding, none of those things dive into the emotional processes each person has to work through for forgiveness. Moreover, each person has a different emotional process given their own family or origin. Given that each person is part of

8. Friedman, *Failure of Nerve*, 37.
9. Friedman, *Failure of Nerve*, 38.

a different system and has different emotional traits and baggage, it makes transitioning out of prison and gaining forgiveness all the more complicated. Furthermore, when we consider the larger context of a general public society, it might even feel impossible. Make no mistake, it is. None of us can work someone else's emotional system. None of us are responsible for how a person responds or reacts to each of us. We are responsible for our actions. Therefore, we cannot go about our actions and not address how our actions have affected these people that are important in our lives.

Attempting to give the participants ownership of this concept, I asked, what is something that, if accused, automatically makes your skin crawl? What is something that you would consider an unpardonable sin against you? Participant A: "I get upset when someone calls me stupid." Participant T: "When I get called a whore." Participant S: "Same here, the whore thing." Participant C: "When people say I am lazy and don't work." So what if one person said these things to you on a normal basis for a great deal of time, but just came up and said he or she was sorry. Would you respond with forgiveness? (All shook their head no.) What would it take for that person to be able to obtain your forgiveness for saying such things that get under your skin so badly? Participant C: "I am not sure." Participant S: "I might be quicker to forgive depending who it was." Participant R: "I am not sure I could give forgiveness. If this person was someone who cared about me and kept saying these things knowing it was upsetting me, and just kept doing it, I am not sure I can forgive." What if the person explained how he or she was terribly sorry for the pain and hurt caused by his or her actions? What if the apology or request for forgiveness came from a deeper understanding of the wrong committed? Part of the issues with obtaining forgiveness is we fail to reframe the issue around how our wrong affected the person. Each of us mentioned things that would deeply hurt us, but it was difficult to process what it would be to forgive someone who has wronged us.

Closing the session I explained that it is impossible to understand and change someone else's emotional processes, including that of forgiveness. However, there needs to be a shift in thinking.

Instead, of focusing on finding the answers in someone else, maybe, we need to consider new questions for ourselves. When we better understand our own emotional processes, it gives us a better understanding of how our actions affect the entire system. When we have a better understanding of ourselves, our own values, our own emotions, and irritations, we can be a calm presence and effect an entire family and social system in a positive way.

Low and High levels of Self-Differentiation

In order to understand ourselves better we need to improve our level of self-differentiation. "Differentiation means the capacity of a family member to define his or her own life's goals and values apart from surrounding togetherness pressures, to say 'I' when others are demanding 'you' and 'we.'"[10] I asked the question: Have any of you ever had to hide a part of yourself or conform something about you to be able to be close to a spouse or loved one? (most nodded heads yes) Ronald Richardson states, "To be able to identify and pursue what you want for yourself while maintaining a close relationship with each other is one of the major goals of family of origin work."[11] This is not stubborn determination to be right despite evidence. Instead, it allows each of us to hold a position about something and be open to the differences of others. "It does not think change is an admission of inadequacy."[12]

Self-differentiation happens in high and low levels. "People range from high levels of differentiation to low levels on a hypothetical scale, depending how much basic self (or non-negotiable self) is present."[13] The key to this work is to raise the low levels of differentiation and reinforce the healthy levels of differentiation. The low levels of differentiation are often called "fusion." Ronald Richardson spends some time in his book *Family Ties that Bind*

10. Friedman, *Generation to generation,* 27.

11. Richardson, *Family ties that bind,* 36.

12. Richardson, *Family ties that bind,* 36.

13. Gilbert, *Extraordinary relationships,* 18.

talking about unspoken rules of the family.[14] Often these unspoken rules are where are the lowest levels of differentiation. These unspoken rules create the highest amount of anxiety. These unspoken rules cause either ourselves, our loved ones, or our social system to react in a highly anxious or sometimes toxic way.

To create discussion on the topic of low levels of self-differentiation, I asked: Have any of you ever had to adjust a value or goal to save an argument? Participant B: "I gave up the goal of owning my own auto shop. Even though I worked very hard and saved a bunch of money for the start-up costs, my wife was against it. I knew it would be hell to pay even though it was my money." Participant R: "Mine is small, but I watch TV shows my ex-wife wants because when I don't she thinks I just don't make any effort." Participant A: "I want to have the ability to go out with my friends, but my wife is always challenged thinking I don't love her and want to spend time with other people besides her. That is not the case and I always tend to give in." Have any of you ever gave in to pressure by reoffending? Most nodded yes.

Then I asked: What are some things that each of you are unwilling to give in? Participant K: "I won't give in regarding sexual stuff." Participant A: "Me either." Pressing the discussion, I asked: Has anyone ever challenged your sexual identity? Participant K: "My family hasn't but when I was in prison, I got into a fight over someone trying stuff on me." So in that instance, he challenged a non-negotiable to you. Is there anything else that is non-negotiable? Participant J: "My kids. I mean, I don't have custody, but I always love them and always want what is best for them." Participant T: "Yea, same here. My kid is far away, but I will always love her." Participant C: "I have issues when someone challenges my manhood. Like, if someone says I cannot take care of my family, or someone says I wasn't man enough to handle my woman. In prison, I would go so far as getting in a fight for someone who called me a bitch." Participant K: "Yeah, the fact that I am a man never escapes me and will always be. I will always dress like a man, work like a man, and act like a man."

14. Richardson, *Family ties that bind*, 12–14.

Low levels of self-differentiation can get us to react in an unhealthy way. For example, Participant C, you mentioned you would get in a fight if someone called you a bitch. Participant K, you mentioned you got in a fight for someone approaching you in a homosexual manner. We all have our own unspoken rules. However, what are the rules for our families? Participant R: "Don't talk back to momma. Even if she is wrong, just acknowledge and then walk away. But, if you talk back to momma, the entire family sees it as disrespect and she takes it as a personal challenge." Participant T: "My family has this status quo for the neighborhood, kinda like a neighborhood standard. They just don't want to be embarrassed by my actions."

What about the bigger picture? What are some unspoken rules for each of your larger social structures, such as your friends? Participant A: "Be a man, do manly stuff." Participant K: "Work hard and your weak if you cry or ask for handouts." Participant S: "Be a lady and don't talk about sex." Participant T: "Be the step-ford wife and mother." Participant J: "Never lose your kids." Participant C: "Don't be gay." Participant R: "Don't get caught." What happens when these rules get broken? Participant S: "You are shamed as a whore with no morals." Participant J: "No one has any sympathy for you if you lose your kids. Even if it was for the best for them to go elsewhere." Participant T: "Yeah, you almost get a scarlet letter of shame and embarrassment if you don't have custody of your kids."

Moving the discussion to higher levels of self-differentiation, I explained that the idea of being self-differentiated at a higher level is when it seems you have that scarlet letter or shame present, you still function at a higher level. It is almost as if you let it bounce off you like teflon. The idea here is to be goal-directed despite opposition.[15] "Being goal directed means that you are able to clarify your own values and decide what is important to you."[16] This does not mean to disregard relationships. Instead, it creates healthy relationships with fewer problems. "In contrast to the goal-directed person is the relationship-oriented person, who is less emotionally

15. Richardson, *Family ties that bind,* 12–14.
16. Richardson, *Family ties that bind,* 12–14.

mature. For the less emotionally mature, it is crucial for people to like and foare for them and it is catastrophic when people don't."[17]

I asked, Is it possible to not really care what people think? Participant S: "Depends on who it is." Participant K: "Yeah, if I barely know you, I really don't care what you think about me." What if it is someone you care about, say your mom, dad, girlfriend or boyfriend? Participant S: "I definitely care what my boyfriend thinks about me." Participant B: "I care about what my kids think of me." Do any of you let it guide how you act or react? Participant B: "I have given my kids money when I really didn't have it to give because I wanted them to know I love them." When I asked, "Do you feel like you are able to make rational decisions thinking through the pros and cons, or do you react purely on feelings?" Almost all unanimously answered feelings.

Closing the session, I explained that sometimes reacting or functioning through feelings of others can create a hostile environment. Yet, when we react to these people's feelings, especially when our reaction is more criminal behavior, "we are lowering the other person/system's pain thresholds, helping them to avoid challenge and compromising the mobilization of their nerve."[18] However, sometimes resisting our system's anxiety, or in some cases sabotages to resist change are difficult.

Sabotage

Opening the session, I explained that there are typically two reactions when a system gets difficult or highly differentiated. The first is sabotage. This is not an intentional set up for failure. In this instance, it would be creating an emotional response to get you to function or react the way they want you to. For example, I used to get all bothered when I was called fat. I used to be in shape so to be called fat was a great insult. I would get incredibly upset and defensive. After learning about this process, I learned it was one

17. Richardson, *Family ties that bind*, 12–14.
18. Friedman, *Failure of Nerve*, 144.

of my emotional "buttons." Therefore, I worked to change it. Now when someone calls me fat, I thank them for the public service announcement. I still have others but the point is we all have buttons or areas where those closest to us can easily sabotage us into thinking on a high anxiety or emotional scale.

Have any of you recognized any attempts to sabotage or "buttons" of your own? Participant S: "Being called a whore." Participant A: "Being called a dope head or idiot." These are some of the same phrases we talked about before. Such as fighting over challenges over sexuality and manhood. However, each of these create an emotional reaction.

The other emotional reaction is for a relationship to triangle. This is when a third party, could be a person or a thing, is brought in a relationship between two people. Usually, when anxiety gets too intense, people triangle. This does not mean that triangles are good or bad. Triangles are just a part of the relationship system. "Triangles are ubiquitous and automatic in emotional systems. They are considered to be the molecule or basic building block of any system of people. The goal is not how to get out of them, however, but rather how to manage in and through them."[19] The most common is that of an affair or the parent child triangle. When things get unstable in a marriage relationship, bring in someone who better understands, brings spark, or whatever is lacking. This is an unhealthy triangle. However, I want to be careful distinguishing between healthy and unhealthy or good and bad, because triangles are just part of the system and they can adjust into both of those fashions at any given moment of anxiety in the system.

Triangles are just part of the system. They are everywhere. We are all part of them and have them within our system. The key here is recognizing roles in triangles. "There are three basic roles in triangles and their coalitions. There are prosecutors, victims, and rescuer."[20] There are obvious exceptions to this rule. There are times when the roles are different. However, these are the usual roles. "Though it is still a sign of fusion in the system when

19. Gilbert, *Extraordinary relationships*, 77.
20. Richardson, *Family ties that bind*, 67.

members take on these roles, it is healthier when every member can play all the roles equally well."[21] I asked: Do any of you want to be in a relationship where you always have to be the bad guy? (All shook head no) Do you want to be in a relationship where you are always saving the day and rescuing from trouble? (All shook head no) Based on these answers, I would assume no one wants to always be a victim either. (All agreed)

Working to flesh this concept out, I asked, can any of you think of the triangles in your system and how they increased or decreased problems? Participant K: "The ones I am thinking of created more problems." Participant A: "For me, I always triangled in drugs, which created more problems." Participant S: "Yeah, I did the drug thing too." Think of other triangles, maybe where someone triangled you into their relationship. I am sure you wanted to be helpful, but did it help or cause more trouble? Participant B: "Yeah, a friend of mine ended up confiding in me about problems with her boyfriend, so she and I had sex." So it hurt her other relationship. What are some times when the triangle worked? Participant K: "I got with both my parents needing some help on some stuff and they helped me out." Do you think you owe them anything for this help? Participant K: "Absolutely." There is another triangle, you, your parents, and the debt you owe. Do any of you have siblings? Participant C: "Yes, I have 3." Tell me about the sibling rivalry. Participant C: "yeah, I could see a lot of triangles in that." Usually, within the sibling rivalry triangles people gain identities, such as the good child, the black sheep, the jokester, and so on. Did any of you get some of that? Participant S: "Yeah, I am the only one in my family that went to prison, so I fall in the black sheep category." How did that affect your identity? Participant S: "I just knew I was going to have to be a loner." Participant T: "Yeah, I figured the same."

Closing the session, I explained that recognizing our "buttons" and triangles in our social and family systems help us recognize our own functioning. We can also see how our anxious habits form. Such as, what really gets us upset? Who is our go to person

21. Richardson, *Family ties that bind*, 67.

when our kids are acting up? Who do we go to when our girl-friend, boyfriend, or spouse is on our case about something? What causes us to go to that person? When our friends come to us, what are they expecting us to do? There are many more questions we can recognize about triangles. However, we must recognize that we all have "buttons" and we are always in a triangle and we just have to know how to function within it.

FUNCTIONING WITHIN DYSFUNCTION

My closing remarks for the focus group was to summarize all our discussion points and cover the topic of functioning despite all kinds of dysfunction. I explained that every family and social system has a certain level of dysfunction. All of us have our stories about how our respective families and friends are dysfunctional. Unfortunately, sometimes that dysfunction can get in our way and influence us to go back to previous destructive behavior. When we do we throw off the entire social and family system again which in turn creates more problems. Unfortunately, we have to realize that we have wronged a system. The system was off balance when we came out of prison. "We are not adequately prepared to reintegrate with the family system's expected roles for our return, such as care-giver, breadwinner, and relationship partner."[22] Instead, we have some work to do to be restored. Restorative justice requires us to do what we can to help the system readjust to our better function-ing. This takes time. "Reintegration stress is an important concept relevant to family and community reentry following release from incarceration. Any assumptions about a family member returning home to the status quo following incarceration are erroneous."[23] Each of our family or social systems undoubtedly became anxious about our return. Therefore, these systems put in some safeguards to adapting. These safeguards involve both triangling and sabotage. Withstand that sabotaging from each system. Keep doing positive

---

22. Stojkovic, *Prisoner reentry*, 100.
23. Stojkovic, *Prisoner reentry*, 116–117.

work. The work is difficult. It is a lifetime endeavor. Dealing with family, adapting to a new way of thinking, functioning on a higher level and being a non-anxious presence when everything else is going absolutely crazy is part of how God is working and has been working through people since the beginning of time. Unfortunately, it is very difficult to see God working when it seems everything from family to social structures are pivoted against every move we make good or bad. Notwithstanding, we have no control over if society will ever fully adapt restorative justice. We have no control over if our family will ever forgive our previous actions and help us reintegrate back into society. However, we can control what we do. When we work through our family and social processes in positive ways, it will adjust the entire system in positive ways.

This is the gospel. Jesus came in a system and walked, talked, and dined with prisoners, outcasts, and rejects of society. He gave them names and status. His life and actions changed the whole world. Jesus atoned an entire society of people by restoring broken people. Jesus is still forgiving and atoning for each of us. Therefore, keep doing God's work. Keep working through this complicated family process stuff because society will fight back but will eventually adapt to you being a productive member of society.

The remaining participants responded positively to the talk. One participant questioned how long will it take to really change anything? I reminded him that he is only responsible for changing himself and the system will have no choice but to adapt. Participant S asked how to get other jobs to recognize her efforts. I explained that unfortunately, we have no control over our social and family systems. There are a lot of flaws in the social system. It is definitely retributive. However, I offered to help any of the remaining participants any way I can to help them be restored back into their communities.

RESULTS

Unfortunately, there was a lot of material about systems theory that was more advanced than many of the participants could understand. This created confusion. Moreover, many attempted to use systems theory as a way to trick people into treating them how they wanted. When this did not work, some dropped out. There was some improvements to some of the participants relationships and work life. A couple of people really understood what was being conveyed and it showed slight improvements in lifestyle. Two participants reoffended and were unable to complete the project and two others simply quit coming.

In a number of ways, the project confirmed my hypothesis. Many people reoffend due to low levels of self-differentiation. All the participants had stories of their friends, family, or co-inmates who tried to "do right" but their anxiety got the best of them. Two of the participants of the focus group did reoffend after having arguments with their significant others. Men are commonly sabotaged into reoffending by challenges to their manhood, such as homosexuality, ability to provide, sexual performance, and overall masculinity. The focus group conversations from the male participants about their friends and co-inmates/parolees revealed that when these issues arise, it creates high anxiety. The most common issue that arose was from the homosexual issues in prison. Four of the five male participants admitted to being approached or having some sort of altercation in prison about homosexuality. All the male participants in the focus group explained a great fear or homophobia about being approached while in prison. It did not matter if there was homosexual tendencies while incarcerated or not, this was an issue that raised issues of anger, and hostility. The second was challenges to the male inability to provide or make a lot of money. Three of the five participants in the focus group discussed the struggles to provide for their significant other or children. Most worked in construction or low level paying jobs. Only one participant was currently working in construction, but two that were unemployed had worked in the business awhile. The other two, while employed, were not making enough money to survive. While the construction work paid good, it took a hard toll on the male body, and if it rained or weather did not permit, pay was lacking. Therefore, many would steal, rob, or burglarize to create a pseudo presentation of success. The legal implication were of no matter when considering image and reputation. Hopefully, the three remaining men understood that they can control how they respond to these challenges and none of those things change their maleness.

Women are commonly sabotaged into reoffending by challenges to the number of their sexual partners, or their motherhood. In the focus group, two of the three women commonly expressed struggles about motherhood and losing custody of their children. All three women in the focus group discussed challenges concerning promiscuity. These areas create high anxiety in women. Unfortunately, due to the legal consequences of past actions, all of the women that began the focus group did not have custody of their children. This created anxiety within them throughout the entire project. Unfortunately, the two women who had children did not complete the project. One reoffended and the other disappeared. Yet, both addressed how they were constantly considered a bad mother simply because they lost their kids. It was difficult to address the anxiety because there was a considerable amount of hurt, guilt and shame. However, all of them also struggled with accusations of promiscuity. All of them struggled as the men were challenged that they should have sex with more and more women but the women were troubled by constantly be considered a whore. So, all of them felt that if they were going to be called a whore, why not use it for their advantage and get what they want out of it. Many had issues understanding their own sexual identity. Sex was currency and could provide whatever drug and service they wanted. Hopefully, the project helped the sole remaining female to understand her own sexual identity.

While the project confirmed my hypothesis, I am not sure during its short tenure, it helped any of the participants make seismic shifts. Systems theory is a lifetime endeavor. Furthermore, all the participants struggled with the systems issues of mental health, drug problems, and there was a severe lack of education. These issues limit society's ability to restore, even if it wanted too.

Accordingly, the lack of time, understanding, and addresses to drug and mental health issues, severely limited this projects ability.

CONCLUSION

Each person that was part of the focus group has committed a crime. Each person was sentenced and was incarcerated through ADOC. Unfortunately, not everyone who started the project/focus group finished the project. Many felt God did not care for them. However, each of them were created in God's image with thoughts, feelings, and mannerisms. St John of Kronstadt said, "Never confuse the person, formed in the image of God with the evil that is in him, because evil is but a chance misfortune, illness, a devilish reverie. The very essence of the person is the image of God and this remains in him despite every disfigurement."[24]

24. Quotation found in Bell, *What we talk about* ,218.

CHAPTER 4

Evaluations and Conclusions

IN THIS CHAPTER I will review several aspects of the project. I will explain the research method utilized for this project. This will include an understanding of qualitative research and measurements. Moreover, understanding ethnography and how it builds and guides theology and can be used for pastoral care will be revealed as a driving force for this project's shape, measurement, evaluation, and conclusions. I will reveal some reflections based on my observations about the focus group's participation, attention, understanding, and embedded theology and how it affected the project. I will address some improvements or a stronger understanding of restorative justice and the social gospel. Moreover, challenges, highlights, and limits of this ethnographic study will be reviewed. Finally, I will conclude with a summary of the project and some observations. Therefore, this chapter will address the research method, a new understanding of ethnography, a stronger understanding of restorative justice and the social gospel, an enlightening understanding of limits of this study of people struggling to transition back into society, and conclude with some observations and summary.

RESEARCH METHOD

In the ADOC, upon arrival, there are various tests and interviews a person goes through. These are very controlled, and precise. This allowed them to gain some precise measurements and numbers concerning someone's risk of violence, education level, and security threat. However, this project could not utilize such a practice. This project required an ethnographic study. "In strong contrast to quantitative protocols and reports, ethnography values a very different kind of data—often discovered through disciplined attention to a few research sites or participants."[1]

The goal of this project was to draw upon systems theory and the social gospel to address some of the problems people face transitioning out of prison. Generally speaking, the project achieved its goal. However, the method utilized for the communal contextual pastoral care was family systems theory, and working through family process is a lifetime endeavor. Therefore, I could not quantify success from the limited time within this project. Roberta Gilbert, in her book *Extraordinary Relationships,* talks about levels of self-differentiation, explains, "Most people remain at the level of differentiation attained by the time they left home. Improvement is possible, but with hard work. However, only a small increment of change is possible after leaving one's original family."[2] Moreover, there was a significant understanding barrier among the participants of the focus group to many of the concepts. The project followed a program outline to provide introductory material to get people to understand and grasp the larger picture and how sin and criminal behavior affects the entire system. Unfortunately, one participant wanted to use this as ways to manipulate people into doing or acting a certain way. There were considerable improvements in a few participants lives and actions. The one female participant had expressed how her relationship with her boyfriend improved and she was promoted at her company. Another participant talked about how his family life improved and he is growing closer to

1. Scharen and Vigen, *Ethnography as Christian theology,* 5.
2. Gilbert, *Extraordinary relationships,* 25.

God. There were also people who dropped out of the program or did lack luster work. Accordingly, this work utilized ethnographic study and measured data on a qualitative basis.

A project that wishes to introduce a new philosophy of life and thinking, will have its challenges. All the participants of the focus group expressed that they were set in their ways of thinking. However, one of these challenges is the person's mental instability. Five of the eight participants stated they should be on some sort of psychotropic medication but refused to be on them. Further, certain adults have a difficult time grappling with changes in thinking and belief. This challenging changes were often met with hostility. Not that any of the people in the focus group were violent, some had a history of violence, but there was a great deal of animosity toward some of the issues addressed in this project. Further, these men and women live unstable lives including unstable work, unstable money, and unstable relationships, all of which are systems factors addressed through this project. Thus, a few participants dropped out and did not complete the project. Measuring results quantitatively was not possible. However, there was another way to assess results. Mary Clark Moschella says, "Ethnography is a way of immersing yourself in the life of a people in order to learn something about and from them. Ethnography as pastoral practice involves opening your eyes and ears to understand the ways in which people practice their faith."[3] This study proved slightly difficult. I have experience with criminal behavior. I have been through the ADOC. Lastly, I transitioned out of prison and with time and hard work, done so successfully. Therefore, to immerse myself in the lives of people to learn something I had experienced was quite a challenge. Yet, I had to realize my experience is likely the exception or more of an anomaly. However, I wanted to be like a pastor to these people in this study. Thus I engaged in pastoral ethnography. "When pastors engage as many people as possible in research and then analyze the accumulated data, a fuller picture and its diverse

---

3. Moschella, *Ethnography as a pastoral practice*, 4.

constituents emerges."[4] I wanted to experience the fuller picture and experience the diversity.

Studying people, their lives, and culture to gain a better understanding is quite difficult. "Ethnography is not a simple or linear practice, like walking from point A to point B. Ethnography is more like embarking on a journey, and stopping along the way to see what strikes you."[5] This project had a structured curriculum to introduce and work through family systems theory. However, there was a great deal of flexibility to see where the directed conversations would lead. This is consistent with an ethnographic method. "Ethnographic accounts and explanations are better understood as narratives than as scientific treaties. Ethnographers engage in the communal life of people, gather data and analyze them with honesty and rigor, and then construct accounts of their experiences, their findings, and their conclusions."

In order to engage in the communal life of these people, I needed to gain a full understanding of my own experience with prison transition. When I was released from prison, I had a stable place to go. I had a family that was supportive and helpful throughout the entire time of incarceration, both physically through visitations, and financially. Also, I had a strong work ethic with strong work experience and an education that helped me transition back into society. While I had been to prison and transitioned out successfully, I did so with a great deal of help and privilege. I recognized my story was unique. However, I knew others had a unique story as well. Scharen and Vigen explain, "Ethnography provides a way to take particularity seriously."[6] It allowed me to see how particular my situation was and compare it to theirs. Most people did not receive the normal visitation from family. "Prison and jail visits can be emotionally, physically, and economically difficult activities in which to engage. There is a lack of privacy, restrictions on physical contact, and difficult interactions with staff.[7] Many

4. Moschella, *Ethnography as a pastoral practice,* 14.

5. Moschella, *Ethnography as a pastoral practice,* 19.

6. Scharen and Vigen, *Ethnography as Christian theology,* xxi.

7. Stojkovic, *Prisoner reentry,* 112–113.

people were unable to speak to their family through the collect call system. Therefore, most felt abandoned and alone. Most did not receive stable financial support while incarcerated. Therefore, most of the people in my focus group experienced completely different circumstances, feelings, and obstacles than my own while incarcerated. Moreover, upon release, many did not have a stable home. A few had to go to a homeless shelter, some did go live with parents but those situations were far more unstable than mine. The last few had to live with friends or hotels until obtaining a stable living situation. None of the participants had the educational background I did, though, some did have good work ethics and a decent work experience. Several worked in construction and finding employment wasn't incredibly difficult. However, for the female participants, finding employment was a struggle. While, I had some struggles gaining employment, it was not long after release, I was working. While the men may have obtained employment, it was highly unstable, and the women had a very difficult time.

These and many others helped me understand that my transition experience was likely the exception and not the rule. As already discussed, I know what prison ministry consists of in Alabama. I knew it was not sufficient for my transition needs. Therefore, it was even more lacking for people who had less support and privilege than me. Therefore, the goal of this project is to minister to those that no one wants to really minister. I wanted to get to know these people and their struggles. I wanted to help people work through these challenges. However, what I really wanted to determine was a reason for recidivism. Why do people go back? I do not think anyone wants to go back. Unfortunately, I think people get stuck in an emotional cycle and due to a poor understanding of emotional process. I called it a failure of nerve.

The most reasonable way to test my hypothesis given the parameters of my project was this ethnographic study. I knew restorative prison ministry in a retributive setting would be messy and difficult. I knew the ethnographic study would be arduous. Clark explains, "Ethnography is a complicated, messy, and humbling endeavor. The main reason for doing this work is to add some knowledge to one's understanding of a group or a particular religious practice."[8] Researching, engaging, and working with people with criminal and troubled pasts was incredibly challenging and certainly messy. Throughout the study, I pressed each participant to be as candid as possible. I wanted to see all the emotional processes no matter how unhealthy it may be. "Ethnographers strive to probe the diversity of cultural, social and religious practices and attitudes in a community in a non-judgemental way."[9]

All the participants had a view of God that was in many cases unhealthy. Initially, seven of the eight participants of the focus group, when surveyed about God, answered either conventionally good answers or answers to buy their time in the focus group. However, through discussion, six of the eight participants thought God was either cruel or a bully that did not care about them. Only one was attending a church on a regular basis. The one church attended or frequently visited is quite large, very contemporary, and offers a food ministry. However, none of the participants really felt they should go. Most felt they were beyond whatever God had to offer. However, much of the driving force to not attending church boiled down to lack of desire. They felt unwelcomed, lacked understanding of what was really being said, felt overwhelming judgement from a crowd, and had no desire to go.

RESTORATIVE JUSTICE

The approach for this study was to create an encounter with restorative justice. Unfortunately, Alabama follows a retributive justice philosophy. One could easily observe that the population of Alabama agrees with retributive justice. There is a great desire to see punishment. Sadly, a cursory look at the comments section of a local news story about someone's criminal behavior will reveal an attitude of people who lack understanding of what is cruel and unusual punishment. Further, the general population is unconcerned

8. Moschella, *Ethnography as a pastoral practice*, 32.

9. Moschella, *Ethnography as a pastoral practice*, 35.

and unsympathetic to someone working to transition out of prison. Unfortunately, this type of thinking was embedded in some of the participants of the focus group. Three of the eight participants felt they did not deserve a better life. Instead, they agreed that they should be punished. Notwithstanding, "countless Americans agree that the criminal justice system is broken and that many aspects of it violate human dignity."[10] All the participants of the project agreed that the system within Alabama is broken. The ADOC seems very intentional about dehumanizing the people that go through its gates. People are given an AIS (Alabama Inmate System) number. This number is an identifying marker. The people are served food that is sub-par. The living conditions are treacherous. Lastly, the ADOC has been sued for unethical practices by its guards for mistreatment of inmates.[11] Each participant had stories about their experiences in prison that were demeaning and humiliating. They all spoke about how intentional these practices were. People feel that wrongdoing must be punished. However, retributive justice in the Alabama and the ADOC has not reduced crime, and not slowed prison overcrowding.

This project introduced a different approach. I wanted to see how a restorative justice approach would affect the lives of the participants in my study. Morneau explains, "Restorative justice is a way of responding to harm that focuses on repairing relationships and healing all those who are impacted by crime."[12] This approach addresses both the victim who was hurt and the person who committed the crime. Moreover, restorative justice addresses all parties involved and works to not dehumanize the person who commited the crime. Some of the participants in the focus group felt that their crimes did not have a victim. However, through the work of systems theory, each had to address how their wrong doing affected an entire system, including their family. This was enlightening to the participants. Four of the eight participants talked about how they never considered how their crimes caused hurt to their

10. Morneau, *Harm, healing, and human dignity*, 3.

11 Tutwiler Prison for Women: Widespread Sexual Abuse.

12. Morneau, *Harm, healing, and human dignity*, 3.

family. However, addressing the hurt victims is only half of restorative justice. It gives human dignity to all parties. In a pastoral letter, the United States Conference of Catholic Bishops said:

> "A Catholic approach begins with the recognition that the dignity of the human applies to both victim and offender. As bishops, we believe that current trend of more prisons and more executions, with too little education and drug treatment, does not truly reflect Christian values and will not really leave our communities safer. We are convinced that our tradition and our faith offer better alternatives that can hold offenders accountable and challenge them to change their lives; reach out to victims and reject vengeance; restore a sense of community and resist the violence that has engulfed so much of our culture." [13]

This project was to restore some lost humanity and create the alternative the council of Bishops wrote about. This was especially important to the female participants. All of them struggled with their sexual behaviors both before incarceration and after release. They each felt objectified, less than human and only good for someone's sexual pleasure. The men participants were more guarded about their guilt and shame. One would talk about how everyone is treated like animals, so it should be expected that they will continue to act like animals outside of prison. However, in order to do so, restorative justice provides a broader picture of how sin creates harm and how much harm affects the entire system. The participants of the project needed to see how their actions would hurt others and themselves. This principle became real when two of the participants reoffended. The remaining group was affected. "Restorative justice calls us to see crime, and harm in any form, as a violation of people and relationships rather than solely a violation of law."[14] Therefore, this project integrated how crime affects the entire family process. I engaged each participant on how their family and social system reacted when they were incarcerated. We discussed the challenges their system endured upon their return.

13. Morneau, *Harm, healing, and human dignity,* 5–6.
14. Morneau, *Harm, healing, and human dignity,* 6.

I asked and engaged the participants to notice the anxiety they created on their social and family systems. I wanted them to see they didn't just break the law. They harmed an entire system, but also themselves.

Yet, where retributive justice stops at who broke the law and how must they be punished, restorative justice sees the whole picture. We engaged in how to heal the harm created to the entire system. "It is important to remember that every person is more than the worst thing they have ever suffered or done."[15] The project brought to light how each participants system is constantly adjusting to both good and bad things. One of the participants saw adjustments to how her family was treating her, and was excited to announce a promotion at her job, which in turn provided more money. Another participant attempted to utilize this system adjustment to manipulate people to react how he wanted. He would talk about how he would upset his mother on purpose to get her to give him money. We discussed how the system adjusted while they were incarcerated and the challenges to the adjustments. These challenges included financial contribution, known as "putting money on their books." The challenges of the collect calls to stay connected. Finally, the challenges of travel to visit the participants. All revealed how troubling their incarceration was to their family. There was an agreement that incarceration is partially a tax on our loved ones. However, the discussion continued addressing how the system had to adapt again to each of their returns. Sometimes recognizing something happened is the first step to creating healing. Most of the participants had never considered all the troubles their family endured during their incarceration and the changes made upon their release. We addressed when the changes are unhealthy. We discussed how the system may intentionally or unintentionally sabotage to create the old normal again.

Part of the restoration is to resist the sabotage from the system. In order to do so, we discussed a stronger understanding of self. A major component of systems theory is self-differentiation. As stated, my hypothesis concerning recidivism was that people

15. Morneau, *Harm, healing, and human dignity*, 20.

functioned on lower levels of self-differentiation and when anxiety is high, they do not react in healthy ways. I explained this as a failure of nerve. Working with the participants we discovered trigger points. These were phrases or actions that would create an anxious response. The most common for the men participants was the comments or actions that emasculated, or challenges to their sexual identity. One of the male participants spoke about being called a "bitch" upsets him so much, he would become violent. Another talked about being called "stupid." Two men talked about how upsetting it was when someone would joke about their sexuality. The most common for the women participants were those that challenged their effectiveness as a mother and history of promiscuity. Two of the female participants suffered a great deal of guilt and shame about not having their kids. Unfortunately, these same two participants did not complete the project. All of the female participants spoke about their use of sex to obtain money, drugs, or whatever was needed. Therefore, all talked about how upsetting it was to be called a "whore."

These attempts or successful sabotages from the social or family system would create a trauma in the participants. These people felt a great deal of hurt because it seemed the people they loved did not want them to succeed. All of the participants spoke about how hurtful it is when their family and friends seemingly turn against them. However, this was often not the case. The system was simply resisting adjustment. Yet, "one of the reasons that restorative practices are so powerful is because they can play in important role in the process of trauma healing in both victims, offender, and community."[16]

Unfortunately, this project did not get to address a major need for the community to get involved in the restoration of the person coming back into society. We as a group talked about how the system will adjust to their own personal changes, however; there needs to be talks about how the overall system can work to restore offenders. Unfortunately, the retributive justice system works in a vacuum of punishment. For non-violent drug

16. Morneau, .Harm, healing, and human dignity, 13.

offenders they are ineligible for most public assistance. "Barred from public housing, discriminated against by private landlords, ineligible for food stamps,[17] forced to 'check the box' indicating a felony conviction on employment applications for nearly every job and denied licenses for a wide range of professions, people find themselves locked out of the mainstream society and economy—permanently."[18] This project focused on the only person each participant can control, which was themselves. However, given the great amount of challenges these people face, society will need to adjust and accept these people. Therefore, efforts need to be made to help offenders restore their right to vote, if they have lost rights. I did not address voting rights and the importance of voting within this project. However, if there will be any adjustments in the system, legislative changes must be made. It is incredibly difficult to succeed if a person is legally discriminated against for living, employment, and social services. Instead, "all are needed to promote restorative justice."[19] This discrimination that boxes out and blocks off people who have commited crimes, such as the participants in the focus group, it only leads to more crime, more victims, and more harm. Notwithstanding, when society joins an offender, who is attempting to better him or herself, working to heal and make restitution to the victims, the entire society and system becomes better for it.

The participants gained a glimpse of a restorative justice effort. The participants saw how this project was attempting to make their lives better. Each participant explained how they felt that I cared for their well being. They also had to address the hurt they caused to all the parties involved in their crime, including themselves. Two of the remaining participants reported that they were rebuilding strained relationships within their family.

Unfortunately, living in a society that follows a retributive justice system, makes any effort toward restoration twice as

17. In February 2016 Alabama did remedy this distinction allowing drug offenses to receive food stamps.

18. Alexander, *The New Jim Crow*, 94.

19. Morneau, *Harm, healing, and human dignity*, 44.

difficult. However, these men and women saw that restoration is possible and there are people available to help walk them through various troubles without reoffending. All the remaining participants celebrated with me when I was given a full pardon by the state. Consequently, the time constraints and societal differences did not reveal much improvements.

SOCIAL GOSPEL

One of the best ways for society and any system to embark on any change is for it to engage the social gospel. "The social gospel is the old message of salvation, but enlarged and intensified. The individual gospel teaches us about the sinfulness of every human."[20] The individual gospel is the only gospel these men and women were presented while in prison. These people felt the church only cared to save their eternally damned soul. However, this does not present the entire gospel. One participant asked, ok now that I am "saved" now what? He wanted to know more. "The social gospel teaches about the sinfulness of the social order and its share in the sins of all individuals within it,"[21] A common fallacy within the social gospel movement is its disregard of the individual sins over the sins. Instead, the social gospel addresses both individual and societal sins. This project wanted to balance between the individual need for reform and through those reformations see how society will adjusts. Unfortunately, there is always resistance to change. Therefore, many would get argumentative toward some of the expanded principles. Two of the participants had a difficult time seeing how helping others had anything to do with the gospel. The social gospel has not been widely accepted, and often falls within a category that is known as "liberalism" in conservative Alabama. Three of the participants participated in prison ministry, lead by conservative groups, and had difficulty reconciling with anything other than the individualistic gospel presented to them.

20. Rauschenbusch, *A Theology for the Social Gospel*, 5.
21. Rauschenbusch, *A Theology for the Social Gospel*, 5.

"The adjustment of the Christian message to the regeneration of the social order is plainly one of the most difficult tasks ever laid on the intellect of religious leaders."[22] This was the case with the participants. They all had imbedded theology about what it meant to be a Christian. For example, the women participants had trouble reconciling their salvation with their promiscuity. Throughout the entire project, they would all apologize after cursing. There was an argument within the focus group because a participant would say "Goddamn" and many of the participants thought that was the unpardonable sin. This theology included consistently going to church, wearing ties, not cussing, refraining from sex. None of their concepts revealed anything close to a healthy theology. It all fell within a very legalistic view of salvation. Overcoming this embedded teaching was quite the difficult task.

Unfortunately, much of the individualistic gospel centers on an escapist mentality. The idea of getting saved to escape hell, damnation, this awful earth and go to heaven. Several of the participants still feared that their various actions would keep them from going to heaven. "The doctrine of the kingdom of God was left undeveloped and mislaid by it almost completely."[23] Instead, this project wished to relay the foundation of what the kingdom of God means here and now. It wished to make the kingdom of God something tangible these people could grasp and understand. The idea that the kingdom of God is some distant far off land that if the proper t's were crossed and i's dotted then all is well, what is the point. "If our gospel is what people think it is, it's no wonder that it's not worth adding church to a busy recreational weekend."[24] Instead, the social gospel reveals God's kingdom here and now. It shows how God is working in each of the participants lives, while they were working with me. Each of the participants had various social needs that if left unattended, they would not have continued participating. Therefore, there was a social worker/networking aspect that helped the participants see the kingdom of God here and

22. Rauschenbusch, *A Theology for the Social Gospel*, 7.

23. Rauschenbusch, *A Theology for the Social Gospel*, 25.

24. Halter and Smay, *The tangible kingdom*, 88.

now. Unfortunately, this was a small introductory effort and time was not in our favor. Notwithstanding, the only way to improve the kingdom of God here and now is to address sin. Sin has to be addressed both individually, as well as socially.

Who is to blame? This is a question for both retributive justice and individualistic salvation. Following an individualistic model, a person has to wrestle with how sin came into this world and what can be done about it. Moreover, there are several different theories of atonement but each present a limited view of who God is and what God has done. The accusation against the social gospel is that it is light on individual sin. "Its teachings seem to put blame for wrong doing on the environment and instead of stiffening and awakening the sense of responsibility on the individual, it teaches him to unload it on society."[25] This is a very limited view of what the social gospel entails. Instead, the social gospel explains how sin has affected the entire society. Sins of greed have created a free market system where only the rich get richer. Sins of self-centeredness has created a society that is harsh and unforgiving. The participants in this project had to come to an understanding as to how their sins affected the entire system. How their social system adapted to them being away and it is readapting to their presence. "The definition of sin as selfishness furnishes and excellent theological basis for the social conception of sin and salvation."[26] Everyone wants things to stay the way it is. Everyone is selfish in what makes them comfortable. It is easy to blame the system for it being built against these people transitioning out of prison. The social gospel would say both the individual and the system he or she is a part of are to blame. However, how can it be addressed and changed?

This project hoped to walk a hypothetical line between addressing individual sin and shaping societal sins. "Societal forces are saved when they come under the power of the law of Christ. The fundamental step of repentance and conversions for systems is to give up monopoly of power and the incomes derived from

25. Halter and Smay, *The tangible kingdom*, 32–33.
26. Halter and Smay, *The tangible kingdom*, 47.

abuse and to come under the law of service. "[27] Unfortunately, the social system, during the time of this project, in northern Alabama was unwilling to give up any power or create fair incomes. Instead, the people of the focus group were still wrestling with jobs. Some of the more "successful" people mentioned that they felt trapped. They didn't mind their job, but it was such a hassle to find a new one. Moreover, the churches these people attended did not help create a network. Often these people would be offered prayers and condolences instead of real help with the challenges they would face. These churches would side with the societal sins that leave people ostracized and left out. Regrettably, much of the time together would be discussing if God really cares about them. If the system and everything is so stacked against them, maybe God is too. Sadly, this project wished to present a liberating social gospel, but the limited time and unstable attendance created a great deal of difficulty.

LIMITATIONS

There were many limitations to this project. The project sought after people just coming out of prison that were considered high risk for return. It did not address the concerns of sex offenders. It did wish to address different sexes and be as diverse as possible. The limitations consist of the issues of race interfering with the presentation, instability of meeting places, inadequate understanding of the materials presented, and instability of the people.

The project started with eight people from various walks of life, and diverse ethnicities and sexes. It was hoped this would provide diverse discussion about the various difficulties people of different races and sexes encountered while transitioning out of prison. Unfortunately, there was a great deal of argument or contest over who had the most difficult challenge. Race is a major theme inside prisons. Most prison gangs are related to race. Therefore, some of the mentality remained. Each person wanted their trek to

27. Halter and Smay, *The tangible kingdom*, 117.

be worse or more challenging than anyone else's. This would present them as the strongest or the expert on challenges. Regrettably, I would have to stifle this conversation every time we met.

We ran into a couple of hurdles around the meeting location. We would start by meeting in an office incubator location that would allow me to use their conference room for free. This lasted only 2 weeks because the owner wanted some sort of rent. We then moved to a coffee shop, which would be where we would meet the majority of the time. It was a nice cozy and secluded which gave us privacy to discuss difficult topics. However, there were individual meetings that would happen at a fast food restaurant, my work office, or wherever we could find a location. However, the unstable meeting place was likely a part of the dropout rate for the participants.

The project intended to use two resources to help people understand the project. The two resources were *A Family Genogram WorkBook* by Galindo, Boomer, and Reagan, and *Becoming Your Best* by Ronald Richardson. I chose *Becoming Your Best* because it was centered around a story. However, it was not well received or understood. Instead, it seemed to create complications from understanding the concepts of systems theory and how it relates to sin and the gospel. Moreover, any references I made to the book would be returned with blank stares, or empty conversations. Therefore, it was quickly dropped as a resource.

This focus group consisted of primarily high school dropouts with little educational or vocational training. There was a definite barrier to learning the materials. For example, when talking about the concept of anxiety, the participants felt this should be treated with Xanax. Moreover, the concept of self-differentiation was often mistaken as stubborn masculinity. Introducing a new way of thinking is difficult. However, there was some understanding. Unfortunately, one of the participants attempted to use the materials in a way to trick or manipulate people to doing other or different things, such as give him money or drugs. The participants understood the system being focused against them, but had a difficult time grasping how their actions affected the system. The idea that they are the only ones responsible for their actions was a difficult issue to understand. Several of them blamed other people for their actions. One participant was a high ranking member of a prison gang, and a high producer in drug sales, while the participant did not want out of the gang, he did want to stop selling drugs and live a normal life.

Lastly, this was research done on people with criminal pasts that were high risk of returning to the ADOC. There is a great deal of instability when doing this research. Several people did not complete the study. Two people returned to jail after being arrested. During their time in the project, they were two of the more lively discussions and would produce what seemed promising improvements. Regrettably, they returned to their previous actions and were revoked on parole so they will be returning to prison. Another participant did not leave. Yet, did not participate or return any of the requested forms to gauge or understand if there was any understanding of the concepts presented. Moreover, if pressed would join discussions but often would be disruptive. Two other participants also left the study. It is rumored of relapses but the deposition of those participants is unknown. These dropouts hindered discussion and severely hindered progress. It was disheartening for the other participants and made discussions quite awkward. I would have to force the conversation and it is difficult to study and let the participants be the experts when I am having to shape and enliven the conversation.

OBSERVATIONS AND SUMMARY

An overall broad stroke of the study would reveal it to be a mixed story. Much was gained and learned by both the participants and myself throughout this study. It helped me recognize the diverse needs of people transitioning out of prison. It brings to light the various different types of dysfunction in both the participants, their families, and the society they are apart. Yet, I was encouraged about the participation. These people want to do better, even the ones who went back to jail. The original course was to stay out of prison. Ultimately, my hypothesis was confirmed. People will reoffend if their anxiety is high in a given situation. If pressed to a corner these people feel there is no other option and no one cares either way. For men, the most common was the challenges to their masculinity and sexuality. For women, the challenges were regarding her motherhood and history of promiscuity. Often, knowing what to do and actually doing that are two seperate things. This was the case often with these participants.

This project had to make adjustments along the way. These adjustments proved to be limitations but also areas of growth. I found meeting at mid-day and providing coffee for the participants went a long way toward their participation. The inconsistency and eventual dropouts did hurt the project. When the focus group was full, the discussion was lively. They were able to bounce ideas off each other and there was always another story to go along with someone else's Unfortunately, toward the end, much of that was directed completely by me. It wasn't that the people were unwilling to discuss. It just was awkward to when the group shrunk down to four.

Attempting to introduce a new way of thinking to a person is difficult. It is more difficult to explain how each person sometimes feeds into the dysfunction of their society or family. This dysfunction often leads to their own recidivism. It is even more difficult to present ideas of a society that restores instead of punishes, when the society they live in loves to punish. However, this project wished to present hope. It hoped to provide a better functioning self, while society and family goes crazy. It hoped to provide a better future.

CHAPTER 5

Highlights, Critiques, and Implications

OVERVIEW

IN THIS CHAPTER, I will present several pictures of what the participants described as prison ministry and what it is like, from their perspective, to be released from prison and the difficulties a person faces. These difficulties include finding suitable employment, finding a reasonable place to live, trying to find social assistance, dealing with a drug problem, and living with a highly dysfunctional family. People will generally send money and help organizations that minister to people while they are in prison. Unfortunately, when these same people are released, they are no longer helped and often abandoned without support. This comes from the assumption that all people who went to prison must have done something really bad. After all, prison is filled with dangerous people who kill over nothing. In reality, prison is filled with people who committed several petty crimes and often could not complete probation or fund their freedom. I wish to address many misconceptions about people coming out of prison and how the current prison ministry model hurts the cause of Christ.

I will then critique this project. I will explain areas that need to be improved. If this will be a lasting model for prison transition ministry, there needs to be several issues worked out. Moreover, a plan needs to be in place to stabilize the participants and provide more structure. I will also discuss weaknesses in the study materials provided and how those materials impeded the study.

Lastly, I will provide how this is proposed toward other parachurch ministries that do work with prisons. There is also a state agency that works with people transitioning out of prison that is interested in the research findings of this project. Furthermore, this project has been introduced to help other churches and ministries that do not focus on prison ministry.

HIGHLIGHTS

Prison transition ministry is about meeting someone where he or she is and helping them acclimate to their society and family systems. Through this project I wanted to gain a different perspective than my own concerning transitioning out of prison. All the participants participated in various prison ministry opportunities. Each person talked about the meaningful relationships created and the wonderful time spent through either the Kairos ministry or various chaplain volunteer opportunities found within the ADOC. One of the participants spoke about how he was the chaplain's assistant, while in prison, so he was able to talk and work with the chaplain in the prison. One of the females spoke about how meaningful one of the church's worship services meant to her. She explained that she never would have made it through her time without the services. Yet, all the participants talked about how each meeting would center around how they each needed to spend more time in their Bibles and how to avoid the fiery pits of Hell. However, each participated because it was an escape from the mundane prison life. It allowed them to associate with other friends who were in other dorms. It also was a place where people could trade goods, albeit illegally, with a different group of people. Upon release, each person had a plan of how things would work out. All the participants expressed that none of their best plans came to fruition. Instead, each was met with more and more obstacles and found out quickly, life outside of prison wasn't what they expected.

All the participants did not end their sentences. Instead, each were released on parole. I contacted a parole officer and presented this project, asking for those classified as high risk to reoffend parolees. These people are under a higher level of scrutiny. Each person has to complete several hours of community service, on top of obtaining employment, and a stable place to live. In the case of these people, the Alabama Board of Paroles would not have released them had they not obtained stable, approved housing. However, they had to maintain and keep the housing or else risk being locked back up for a parole violation. Moreover, each had to report to the parole officer weekly if unemployed and monthly if employed. The participants explained reporting in as one of the more trivial but annoying tasks. Each explained a considerable wait time, which was very problematic for the ones who had jobs. A few of the participants explained they would just take the whole day off because it was easier than asking for a few hours to go report in. Lastly, the participants all talked about how difficult it was to obtain work. While several participants had worked or are working in construction, many discussed how the crews were full, or depending on the season work was slow. However, the others discussed how employers did not consider them for even some of the more demeaning jobs. Yet, each participant had to obtain employment within a reasonable amount of time or risk being sent back to prison for non-compliance and violating parole.

I presented this project as a form of community service that was approved by the parole officer. The parole officer was very enthusiastic about my research and wanted to be as helpful as possible. I explained to him there would be a level of candor about some concerns or struggles within the justice system, such as the report in wait time. However, I explained to him, in front of the participants, that I would not share materials presented that would damage their reputation. I would not report to him if these people were breaking the rules of parole. I wanted him to know that I was not there as an agent of the state to spy out bad behavior. However, I also wanted the participants to know that they were allowed to be candid with me. If the research would be true, it need not be canned answers from people who fear being sent back to prison.

One of the biggest highlights to this project was the insight from the female participants. There is not a lot of resources available to women in Huntsville, AL. Furthermore, there is a great deal of need for many women. Each woman participant struggled with sexual promiscuity. Almost all talked about their drug problems. For them, obtaining drugs was quite easy. One participant talked about never having to pay monetarily for drugs. Instead, she would sell pornographic images of herself. She mentioned that if the money was high enough or if the need was there, she would sell herself in exchange for drugs, or money to pay for a place to stay for the night. However, as sad as that is, after prison, many of her clientele wanted her services again. Her candid conversations of the struggles she had not accepting their offers while she struggles for money was both saddening and enlightening. The other females talked about the same things. One talked about a phrase called, "selling the dream." She would give men the impression of sexual favors and then cheat them out. For her, after prison, was a bit scary. She had cheated a lot of not good people who wanted nothing more than to have sex with her. Each female participant brought a rich display to the conversation about how men dominate society. Each female participant felt shame and said they would be part of the "me too movement" but felt they brought the actions on themselves and were active participants. However, each female participant wanted to create resources for women.

Currently, there are a few homeless shelters that allow women to come and a battered women's shelter called "Hope place" that only police officers and women who have stayed there know the location. Each participant explained that there needs to be drug programs for women. These programs need to be run by women and structured around women. There are a few women's drug recovery programs in Alabama statewide. The largest is known as "Lovelady" in Birmingham Alabama, approximately an hour and a half away from Huntsville. Each participant explained that the Alabama justice system is not built for women and there is not any transition or recovery system in place to help women.

One of the biggest issues women explained that needed to be addressed was in job placement and skill development. Two of the three had not worked in quite some time. Two of the three were married and were homemakers while married. When the marriage fell apart, they were on their own and did not have adequate skills or anything to obtain a decent paying job. There was concerns about parenting. All the participants with kids had lost custody and felt there was no hope of getting them back. However, each participant wanted to know how to be a better mother. They wanted to provide and do what was best for their children, even if that meant their children did not stay with them.

These insights brought to light how even the justice system is geared toward men and how women are left out to fend for themselves. It is true that more men are incarcerated in Alabama than women, but that does not excuse not having adequate resources for women who need help. These women need help obtaining work skills, the ability to recognize and work through toxic relationships, and parenting when necessary. While this project was focused on transition preparation for the entire social system. There was a social work component that helped some of these

My emphasis on the female participants should not discount the joys of the male participant contributions. The male participants brought insights into different struggles. Many were raised under the auspice that the man was the provider for the family. The man made all the decisions, and the man took care of all the problems. These men had a very difficult time wrestling with the fact that they were the man causing problems and all missed the structure the ADOC provided that the free world lacked.

Most were in a construction business. So, they were able to obtain employment that paid better than the female participants. However, their employment had a glass ceiling. They each had hopes of moving up and becoming a general contractor, or even a home builder. However, each knew they felt they would never achieve these dreams. Instead, the highest career goal they might achieve is that of a team lead. Unfortunately, there is not any pay raise to such a promotion. Instead, it just makes a person less likely to be laid off when work gets low. However, not everyone was in construction. There were a few that did have employment problems. These problems consisted of the same issues the female participants encountered, due to lack of skilled training, or lack of consideration because of the criminal background. Therefore, all of them, even those that had decent paying construction jobs, had a lot of trouble meeting ends and providing for their families. This was a definite deterrence to these men's progress and transition. They each expected to come back to society make a lot of money and be able to take care of everything they needed to do. Reality proved to be much different.

The male participants had a really difficult time being not being the "alpha male." In the ADOC, there is a great deal of respect given and received. The atmosphere is a very interesting concept. Part of it is because no one talks about the crimes committed, so no one knows if someone is a terrible murderer, or simple drug abuser. There are rumors and most know who have been there a long time. However, respect is given because no one knows someone's breaking point to get violent. Yet, this was not the case in the free world. The men expected everyone to give them respect because they were the men. Reality proved much different as they found themselves at the bottom of most work structures having to work their way back up. If they had a female partner, she was making all the financial and living situation, especially if they had children. Their friends often disregarded them or poked fun at them because of their prison time. No one took them seriously. Instead, most considered their prison time almost like a vacation. They didn't have to worry about anything, all meals were made for them, they did not have a bill to pay, unless they created it for themselves. Most of the participants friends or social network did not consider going to prison something to be respected. Instead, there was a bit of shame with associating with them. This shame was felt and was a major topic of discussion during this project.

The hardest topic to overcome during this project was the affects each participants crime caused to the entire system. This was especially the case for the men participants. These men wanted to be the problem solvers. They felt people came to them to take care of issues. None of them had ever considered they were problem creators. Each thought they were the one's, even though they were committing various crimes, that people went to for solutions to their problems. These men wanted to be a positive influence to their systems. They love their families. Each wanted to be the best. However, all felt the system was against them so they have no choice but to cut corners and commit the crimes. Notwithstanding, committing crimes always creates more trouble than not. For these men to grasp how much their behavior affected the system was difficult to comprehend.

Lastly, the men participants all wished they had the structure available to them while incarcerated. None actually said those specific words, but there was comfort within the prison system. Each participant knew what to expect. They knew the correctional officers personalities and how to behave when whoever was on shift. They each knew there would be a bed and they knew their dorm mates, both those that stayed to themselves and those considered foolish. There was a scheduled time to eat, a scheduled time for count, and a scheduled time for work. When each transitioned back into society, none of those securities were there. Each person had to make his or her own decisions. The men discussed how having to make decisions for themselves was really a challenge. In the prisons, no matter what they did, they always had a bed. Now, there are house rules that must be followed, or else they can lose their housing and be stuck on the streets. Now the participants had to pay for their food each and every meal. There were responsibilities and no one to make decisions about their lives but themselves.

Each participant went to various chapel services while in prison. All of them participated in some sort of prison ministry while incarcerated. The participants discussed three major critiques of the different programs. The first was all of them were solely focused on salvation. Each wanted to know what else besides saving my sin wrecked soul? Surely, there is more to this Christianity thing then avoiding hell. Secondly, the participants discussed how the relationships while in prison were quite meaningful. They considered the people their friends who came to see them and pray with them and work with them. Yet, all of them felt abandoned and have not been in contact with anyone involved in prison ministry. This was not due to lack of effort on their part, many tried to reach out through various social media platforms, but were unable or shut out. This caused a great deal of hurt. The participants explained that they were only loved by God while they were in prison apparently. However, once they were out, they must have it all figured out. This was the most heart wrenching discussion for me. It does not display love. It does not display grace and is out of the character of God. However, it is difficult to tell people different from what they experienced. Lastly, the participants explained that prison ministry did not do anything besides tell them how to avoid damnation. Many needed network opportunities, resources for coming out, and help getting various social services. Unfortunately, the prison ministry model in the ADOC was inadequate.

MISCONCEPTIONS

In Alabama, there are several misconceptions about people coming out of the prison system. Even more troubling is the misconceptions on how to help people coming out of the ADOC. The most common misconception is that the people that go to prison are hardened criminals. The misconception is that they are vicious and horrible people that do not deserve air. Another misconception is that they are lazy. They go to prison so they can live off the system. The belief is that prisoners get free healthcare and three hots and a cot. None of those are remotely true. However, there are even more misconceptions concerning how people should come back into society. The biggest is that people should just go get a job. It is as if getting a job solves all the problems of life. Another misconception is the lack of remorse or tough love concept. This is the idea that no help at all should be given because they shouldn't have broken the law. Lastly, and likely the biggest misconception is how to address substance abuse or mental health, which are different but sometimes compliment each other.

Entertainment has given people the idea that prisons are filled with terrible people that only wish to rape and kill. "Reagan portrayed the criminal as 'a staring face—a face that belongs to a frightening reality of our time: the face of the human predator.'"[1] The only people that go are dangerous individuals that belong behind bars. These people committed terrible violent crimes. Instead, much of prisons, especially in the ADOC, are filled with non-violent drug offenders. "Convictions for drug offenses are the single most important cause of the explosion in incarceration rates in the United States. Approximately a half a million people are in prison or jail for a drug offense today."[2] There is a complete lack of understanding of the criminal justice system within Alabama. Yes, there are many people incarcerated for violent crimes. However, the ADOC is far overcrowded for various other crimes that usually are non-violent in nature. Unfortunately, one of the best ways to address this misconception is for someone's loved one to have to go. Then people discover that often it is not filled with terrible people who do terrible things. All but two of the participants in this focus group did not have violent crimes. The ones that did have violent crimes felt they were defending themselves or family. They are all tired of being categorized as terrible people. The ADOC is not filled with awful violent people. Instead, it is filled with people who God loves but made some bad mistakes.

No one wants to feel cheated and abused. Yet, one of the most common misconceptions is that prisoners are lazy and only want to live off the system. Many political personalities like to portray both welfare and criminals in the same light. Crime and welfare are used to stir working class whites.[3] The idea is people go to prison and eat, sleep, watch TV, do drugs, have sex with each other and

1. Alexander, *The New Jim Crow,* 49.

2. Alexander, *The New Jim Crow,* 60.

3. For further discussion on political ideologies and crime see Alexander, *The New Jim Crow,*48.

kill each other. None of this is remotely true. In the ADOC, there is a great deal of inmate labor. This consists of being a runner for the prison system, to cutting the grass or working in the kitchen. There are various jobs prisoners have to do but they do not get paid for them. However, almost all of them have incredible work ethics. All the participants wanted to work very hard and provide a decent living for each of their families. None wanted to be a leach on the system. All wanted to contribute to society. They all talked about how their friends felt it was a vacation, when it is not. There is a lot of work that goes on inside the ADOC but none of it is paid. Instead, these men and women do the work because they miss working.

While I do not think people have a remote clue as to what it is actually like in the ADOC, it is more evident of society's ignorance toward their release. In Alabama, there is this folkish idea that someone can pull themselves up by their bootstraps and work their way out of any bind. Therefore, all people who are released from prison should just get to work. The idea that people should just get a job, as if getting a job solves all of life's problems is a common misconception when dealing with people transitioning out of prison. Yes, there is a need for income. However, there needs to be an understanding or addressing the limited nature of someone's income. Martin Luther King Jr. opened a speech saying, "We hold these truths to be self evident, that all men are created equal, that they are endowed by their Creator with certain inalienable rights, that among these are life, liberty and the pursuit of happiness. But if a man doesn't have a job or an income, he has neither life nor liberty. And the possibility for the pursuit of happiness, he merely exists."[4] However, the income of someone has a direct effect on their productivity. Low wages are a constant theme for people coming out of prison. They are banned from obtaining licenses to do various professional tasks. All have a moral turpitude clause that keep people with criminal records from being able to obtain licenses such as real estate or insurance sales licenses, or a license to be an interior designer or cosmetology. Therefore, the answer

4. King, The Promised Land.

is not that these people should get a job. However, society should make pathways for people with criminal records to be able to obtain good sustainable employment with decent wages and benefits.

Alabama does not want to fall in the category of enabling someone to commit crimes. Therefore, many of its citizens hold a very hard stance on crime and criminal justice. Instead of restorative justice, Alabama holds a hard retributive justice stance. Therefore, much of Alabama feel the best way to help someone that has broken the law is punishment. While many people are struggling with food, finances, and housing, the stance people take is that they shouldn't have broken the law. Therefore, life is now forever tough because people who break the law deserve punishment. Unfortunately, this stance is both unsustainable and it violates the constitution. The eighth amendment of the constitution stops people from imposing excessive bail and excessive fines and cruel and unusual punishment. However, what constitutes excessive fines? What is the defining line for cruel punishment. Should punishments be everlasting? The people in my focus group all wondered at what point would it be considered that they did their time? All wondered why is there even limits to incarceration terms if when they get out they are mistreated and ostracized due to their previous criminal record. The problem with this line of thinking is it does not help anyone.

Lastly, most criminal behavior falls under two categories. There is a severe issue with mental health in the ADOC and nationwide issue with drugs. Alabama, like many other states, wishes to criminalize both mental health and drugs. Most of the criminal convictions across the state surrounding drug abuse. However, the only drug rehabilitation or recovery centers available are quite expensive, have very long waiting lists, and have been unsuccessful in addressing the drug problem. Mental health falls within the same category. In North Alabama, there is one center that works off a sliding fee scale to address mental health. Notwithstanding, it takes approximately two months to finally see a medical doctor after initial intake. Surveying the participants of my focus group, all of them at one point during their criminal behavior abused major drugs from cocaine, or methamphetamine. Moreover, all of them also talked about severe mental health concerns such as anxiety, and depression. A few self diagnosed themselves and self treated themselves with various black market pills to ease symptoms. People coming in and out of the prison system often are dealing with drug and mental health problems. Unfortunately, Alabama has yet to move away from punitive justice and sought a solution that gets people the help they need.

CRITIQUE

The goal of this project was to address some of the problems people face when transitioning out of prison drawing upon systems theory and the social gospel. The program introduced concepts of family systems theory integrating restorative justice and the social gospel. The purpose is to help people acclimate back into society and slow recidivism. I hypothesized that people reoffend because of a failure of nerve to withstand sabotage in a high anxiety from family or society not willing to adjust. The purpose of this critique will be to determine if the project was successful, if the method was effective, and how the hypothesis was proved or disproved.

Yes, the project achieved the goal of providing an introduction to systems theory through communal contextual pastoral care. Throughout the program myself, and the group wrestled with several concepts of family systems theory, the gospel and restorative justice. During the time of the focus group, there were changes in how the participants interacted with their families, their attitudes towards the justice system, and slight changes in lifestyles. This report presented edited verbatims revealing how these people grappled with embedded thinking within their own family and social systems. Lasting change is still unknown, yet this project's purpose was to bring an introduction.

The concepts of family systems theory seemed to go beyond the participants level of understanding. The participants had a variety of educational and vocational backgrounds, but none of them had higher education. Therefore, their understanding of the concepts was very elementary. It would have been better had I either used a different terminology than "anxiety" or "self-differentiation" or not even labeled it at all and just lead them through the work. The group would get stuck on such terminology and it limited conversation.

The meeting place created some instability in the program. There was also a change or abandonment of one of the resources. However, the process of working through emotional process remained the same. The objectives used during this project helped reveal how emotional process can and does affect a person's ability to transition back into society. The most engaging part of this program was how limited the current model of prison ministry was to the participants. It was helpful while incarcerated to an extent, but turned hurtful when the relationships were abandoned upon release. The focus group brought incredible insight to the challenges each of them face from economic and social arenas. All wanted to stay out of prison and become assets to society. While some participants did reoffend, the overall consensus was that there was hope for a better, more welcoming society.

The unstable meeting location really made this project very difficult. Some of the participants were not easy to reach. Moreover, having to move from place to place made the project look unsustainable and unserious. The initial meeting place was the most ideal. It was a conference room that while it lacked warmth, it was free from distractions. The coffee shop was generous to allow us to use their space. However, the customers coming in and out, sometimes loud laughter would be a distraction. Moreover, there were books there, and sometimes attractive customers would dissuade the participants. The meeting location needed to be more concrete to create a central meeting location and limit distractions from all the participants.

The project began by providing a two books to each participants. One of them was helpful in working through genograms and providing a larger picture of the social/family system. However, the group did not take any interest in *Becoming Your Best*. It was selected because it presents the principles of family systems theory through a narrative. However, no one read the materials. No one interacted or even engaged in the stories. The book was quickly abandoned. The discussions created a better narrative. The discussions were rich and enlightening. Therefore, moving forward, I would try to utilize videos to help understand the concepts, instead of the book. I would also center the project more on the theological and family reflections that provided very rich discussions.

Lastly, the unfortunate critique is the drop-outs. I was told by a constituent that I cannot take participants failures personally. This is quite difficult. While I celebrated with the remaining participants and the progress each made, my mind goes to the two that re-offended. It causes me to evaluate what areas of their lives did I not consider or work through. Unfortunately, criminal behavior is part of their lifestyle and to change that lifestyle would take more than a couple of months this project worked through. This project presented tools to help people function better. However, not everyone used the tools.

Despite all the troubles and problems this project worked through, the people who participated experienced a more whole gospel. It showed them that God had not rejected them. It also explained that God is still working in each of their lives. God is still gracious, loving, and seeks justice. The participants could see that God wants a more inclusive society. A society that does not condone their wrong doing, but forgives them. The project challenged the participants to be a part of a tangible kingdom of God. It called them to make society better, even if society wasn't interested in their efforts, because God was interested. Therefore, I considered the project an overall success.

IMPLICATIONS

So what is next or how will this project continue? There is still much to be learned while working with people who are transitioning out of prison. There is no cookie cutter program that fits every participant. This project brought incredible insight and broadened my thinking about how people function, and brought out a new level of dysfunction. It created several crises within my theology and thinking. It also helped me be a better pastor to these people. This project had several other positive implications to both the participants, other parachurch ministries, a few local churches, and myself.

The participants were the central focus of this project. While they were in the ADOC, there was a great deal of dehumanizing. The men were treated like animals. The women were treated like pieces of meat. They felt like they were unworthy of any sort of love. The prison ministry did not help this concept when the relationships created seemed to be abandoned. However, this project brought to light several insights. It created relationships and network opportunities. The plan is to continue working with the remaining participants and help them facilitate conversations with other people going through the same struggles. There is also some connections being made with social workers and mental health workers to provide services and resources to these people that are in desperate need. The remaining participants are now actively involved in churches. These churches have been vital in the project's success. None of them have felt rejected. Several have presented their testimony or faith journey. The project helped them see God in a new light. I look forward to continuing to work and walk with them through this spiritual journey.

A major part of this project was a critique of the current prison ministry model within Alabama. This critique realizes there are several limitations and rules concerning the ADOC and what is allowed. However, the largest area of concern was what seemed to be the fickle relationships that were seemingly created. These short term relationships turned toxic to the cause of Christ for the select few that participated in this project. I would bet, it proved toxic for others too. While I never believed this was ever the intention of the prison ministries, they needed to know it was happening.

Therefore, I met with several prison ministry programs, and chaplains that volunteer and work in the ADOC. These people were very positive and receptive toward this project. All wanted to contribute and find whatever was needed to help people get out and stay out of prison. So, many of the prison ministries want to acclimate the materials in this project to an after care program for people they come in contact. So, the prison chaplain or prison volunteer can see how the short term relationships are affecting the inmates. The prison chaplain can slow the toxicity of what is happening before people leave prison.

One of the organizations works primarily in work-release prisons in Alabama. Most of the people within these prisons will either end their sentences or will get paroled out. They are classified as low security. This organization wants to begin working this process while people are still in prison. The leadership wants people to understand and be better prepared for the challenges ahead of them. The expressed concern that many have a "pie in the sky" attitude concerning what it will be like for them. While the ministry does not want to burst the proverbial bubble, it does want to give adequate resources. Therefore, I will be given chapel time, as my schedule allows, to present and recreate this program. There will have to be some adjustments to the structure and there are rules the chaplain has to abide be concerning inmate behavior. However, these details are being worked out.

I do not speak Spanish. However, much of the jail and prison population is an ethnicity other than mine. Yet, much of prison ministry falls in a conservative christian background. Yet, the common hispanic faith is Roman Catholic. Not all Catholics are hispanic. But, there is a need for someone to work with people transitioning out of prison that has the ability to speak the language and comes from the same faith background to help people work through these issues. This project is working with a deacon in Huntsville to seek out prison chaplains or Catholic prison ministries to help people from a Catholic faith and ethnic background to work through the same challenges the focus group worked through.

Much of criminal behavior centers around various substance abuse. There are several programs throughout Alabama that address substance abuse. Some are considered rehabilitation centers because there is medical staff. However, others are considered recovery centers. The rates of success varies and depending on the program. Unfortunately, these programs graduate or provide tools to a lot of men and women, many relapse. What was discovered is that there is a great deal of similarities to the challenges people face transitioning out of prison to those people transitioning out of a halfway house or program. People do not recognize how the family shifted while they were away. People fail to recognize how their drug abuse and sin affects the entire family. These and many other challenges the program director and the executive director wanted to address. Therefore, both wanted to implement a transition program for the drug recovery center in hopes it will slow relapses. Parachurch ministries can move beyond their limited scope, hopefully remove the blinders, that individual salvation is the only way. Instead, parachurch ministries can see the need for the social gospel and how it does not challenge theology, it builds it.

Parachurch ministries are not the only persons interested in this work. The state works through an organization called Lifelink. It's mission states,

> "To bridge the gap between prison and a responsible, productive lifestyle in society that contributes to: 1. Reunification into family and community. 2. A reduction in crime and recidivism. 3. A decrease in victimization. 4. An increase in public safety. 5. A savings to the taxpayer. 6. Development of an untapped workforce."[5]

This program works within one prison in Alabama and does a lot of good. It first works with the families and to help create a healthy atmosphere for people transitioning out of prison. It provides classes to help the inmates gain social skills, job skills, financial skills, and many other tools. The program is doing a version of what this project did. However, it does so in a secular fashion. Therefore, this project worked with the facilitators to help shape and work through it. At the same time, lifelink wants to understand the findings of this research to improve its services and help more people and be more successful. Unfortunately, the program

---

5. LifeLink Career Resource Center Volunteer Opportunities.

is limited to one county and one prison. However, they are seeking more funding and wish to pursue the elements of this project further in other prisons.

This project has been vital to helping churches recognize the image they present about God. I always use the book, *Reading the Bible with the Damned*. The language can be a bit harsh for many traditions, but it is filled with stories of people from ethnic backgrounds that have to wrestle with various challenges from finances to immigration to housing. Much of the church never considered the real difficulties people face leaving prison. Moreover, many have never considered the need for a more liberating theology and interpretation of the Bible. Instead, churches wish to remain comfortable where they are. People with criminal backgrounds are often asked to participate in a "don't ask don't tell" type of format. This means they are allowed to attend and be a part of worship so long as no one knows their past. However, some churches are finding the error in this way of thinking. Instead, they are seeing how God works through people with troubled backgrounds. They are seeing a new sense of grace in the lives of the participants. The participants who have told their story to the churches they attend have enriched the lives of the people in it. Each of those churches evolved and came closer to Christ through their acceptance of the people in this project. Hopefully, many more will follow. Therefore, the local church should see how their rejection of these people affects them. Moreover, the local church will hopefully recognize that God is on the side of these marginalized people. This project helps the local church see ways it can help these people and reveal God's grace in new ways.

Finally, this program had a great effect on me. I began this project with my own experiences coming out of prison. All of my criminal history was non-violent. However, there were still many challenges. Yet, before I made anyone else do this work, I did it myself. I gained incredible insight about myself, a better understanding of my family and their emotional process, and gained a lot of maturity about my situation. Through all this, I was able to obtain a pardon from the State of Alabama for all my convictions. This was an incredible happy ending to a lot of self work.

However, there was more than the good results from my transition. I came to this project hoping to expand my thinking, knowing my experience is different from others. These people who worked with me through this project helped me gain a better understanding of how diverse and troublesome this prison transition problem really is. Moreover, each participant became a friend that enriched my life with their story. We now walk and struggle through this spiritual journey together. However, I was able to see God work through the men and women that participated in this project.

CONCLUSION

Prison ministry in Alabama has been lacking. There are a number of reasons as to why but it falls short of preparing people to leave prison and join society. More is needed for these people than simply sharing the gospel of Christ. One might question if the gospel shared is even the gospel at all, considering some of the responses to the surveys. All the participants surveyed said they believed in God. However, most believed God did not love or care about them. Sadly, this means traditional prison ministry is failing. This project only presented a small step in a broader direction, presenting a social gospel that challenges society to restore instead of punishing. But, it also challenges the person who commited the crime to reconcile with society. Sin exists on both a societal level as well as an individual. Yet, the good news is God still forgives all sins, no matter the level. That is a gospel worth believing in.

APPENDIX 1

The Current State of Prison Ministry in Alabama

I SPOKE OVER THE phone with representatives of four prison ministries in Alabama.

Each discussed issues concerning combining beliefs of multiple volunteers, different views as to what is acceptable and not. Moreover, each explained that the regulations of the ADOC, while broad in stroke offer a wide view of interpretation, creating limitations to prison ministry volunteers.

These limitations are for the volunteer's protection and safety. However, they limit one's ability to build a relationship beyond prison. They limit the level of contact while in prison, such as writing follow-up, or phone calls. A volunteer is only allowed to work within the controlled setting within the ADOC.

Faith Survey Form

To GAIN A BETTER understanding, as to where each participant is coming from, please fill out this form with complete candor. There is no wrong answer and there is no bad judgement for good or bad answers.

What is your view of God?

Were you raised in a church setting or faith tradition? If so, what was it?

Did you participate in any prison ministry programs while incarcerated? If so, which ones and describe your experience.

How has being incarcerated and released changed or affected your faith in God, or lack thereof?

Family and Social System Survey

PLEASE TAKE A MOMENT and provide a glimpse of your family and social life

Who in your family or friends would you consider yourself closest too?

Who in your family or friends would you consider yourself distant?

Do you have siblings? If so, what birth order were you? (first child, middle child, etc)

Are you currently involved with someone? If so, how long?

How did your friends and family react when you went away?

How did your friends and family react when you got out?

Bibliography

Alabama Board of Pardons and Paroles. "Board of Pardons and Paroles." *Annual Report*. 2018. http://www.pardons.state.al.us/Annual_Reports/2017–2018 _Annual_Report.pdf.

Alabama Department of Corrections. *Alaama Department of Corrections*. 2017. Http://doc.alabama.gov/docs/AnnualRpts/2017AnnualReport.pdf. 2018.

Alexander, Michelle. *The New Jim Crow: Mass Incarceration in the age of colorblindness*. New York: The New Press, 2012.

Bell, Rob. *What we Talk about When we talk About God*. New York: HarperOne, 2014.

Biddle, Mark. *Missing the Mark*. Nashville: Abingdon, 2005.

Bowen, Michael Kerr and Murray. *Family Evaluation: An approach Based on Bowen Theory*. New York: Norton, 1988.

Cason, M. *Alabama will build 3 new Prisons*. February 2019. https://www.al.com/ news/2019/02/alabama-will-build-3-prisons-for-men-ivey-announces-do-not-publish.html?fbcli   d=IwARoysinDYkheIRCu1JUP3NV8cll_ S1bQY_xyExWelOa1EbtKsaR5DuzHiJQ.

Cole, G.A. "Justice: retributive or reformative?" *The Reformed Theological Review*, 1986: 5–12.

Duke, H.W. Stone and J.O. *How to Think Theologically*. Minneapolis: Fortress Press, 1996.

Ekblad, Bob. *Reading the Bible with the Damned*. Louisville: John Knox, 2005.

Friedman, Edwin. *Failure of Nerve: Leadership in the Age of the Quick Fix*. New York: Church, 2017.

———. *Generation to Generation: Family process in church and synagogue*. New York: Guilford, 2011.

Galindo, Israel. *Perspectives on Congregational Leadership: Applying Systems Thinking for Effective Leadership*. Richmond: Educational Consultants, 2009.

Gilbert, Roberta. *Extraordinary Relationships: A New Way of Thinking about Human Interactions*. New York: Wiley, 2011.

Gomes, Peter. *The Scandalous Gospel of Jesus*. New York: HarperOne, 2008.

Guthrie, S.C. *Christian Doctrine*. Louisville: John Knox, 2008.

Initiative, Equal Justice. *Tutwiler Prison for Women: Widespread Sexual Abuse by Male Guards.* n.d. https://eji.org/tutwiler-prison-for-sexual-abuse.

James, S.A. "Devine Justice and the retributive duty of a civil government." *Trinity Journal,* 1985: 199–210.

Jr, Martin Luther King. n.d. http://wgbhprojects.s3.amazonaws.com/EYES%20 ON%20THE%20PRIZE/Transcripts/EOTP-204-ThePromisedLand_ TRANSCRIPT.pdf .

Levad, Amy. "I was in prison and you visited me: a Sacramental Approach to Rehabilative and Restorative Criminal Justice." *Journal of the Society of Christian Ethics,* 2011: 93–112.

Lifelink Career Resource Center. *Lifelink Career Resource Center Volunteer Opportunities.* n.d. www.volunteermatch.org/search/org100259.jsp.

Monroe, S.N. Craigo-Snell and S. *Living Chrisitianity: A Pastoral Theology for Today.* Minneapolis : Augsburg Fortress, 2009.

Morneau, Caitlin. *Harm, Healing, and Human Dignity.* Collegeville: Liturgical, 2019.

Moshella, M.C. *Ethnography as a Pastoral Practice: An Introduction.* Cleveland: Pilgrim, 2008.

National Council of the Church of Christ. *Women in Jail and Prison: a training manual for volunteer advocates.* Washington DC: National Council of Churches of Christ, 1988.

Pfeil, M.R. "A Theological Understand of Restorative Justice." *Journal of Moral Theology,* 2016: 159.

Ramsay, Nancy. *PAstoral care and counseling: Redefining the paradigms.* Nashville: Abingdon, 2004.

Rauschenbusch, Walter. *A Theology for the Social Gospel.* New York: Abingdon, 2017.

Richardson, Ronald. *Family Ties that Bind: A self-help guide to Change through Family of Origin Therapy.* Bellingham : Self-Counsel, 2007.

Smay, H. Halter and M. *The Tangible Kingdom: Creating Incarnational Community: The Posture and Practices of Ancient Church Now.* San Francisco: Jossy-Bass, 2008.

Stephenson, Byron. *We need to talk about Justice.* 2012. https://www.ted.com/ talks/bryan_stevenson_we_need_to_talk_about_an_injustice/transcript? referrer=playlist-11_must_see_ted_talks&language=en#t-423138.

Stojkovic, S. *Prisoner Reentry: Critical Issues and Policy Directions.* New York: Palgrave Macmillan, 2017.

Vigen, C. Scharen and A.M. *Ethnography as Christian Theology and Ethics.* London: Continuum, 2011.